GIFT WRAPPING

& GREETING CARDS

GIFT WRAPPING

& GREETING CARDS

Creative ideas for personalizing gifts and cards

Edited by Lydia Darbyshire

CHARTWELL
BOOKS, INC.

A QUINTET BOOK

Published by Chartwell Books
A Division of Book Sales, Inc.
114 Northfield Avenue
Edison, New Jersey 08837

This edition produced for sale in the U.S.A. its
territories and dependencies only.

ISBN 0-7858-0700-4

This book was designed and produced by
Quintet Publishing Limited
6 Blundell Street
London N7 9BH

Creative Director: Richard Dewing
Designer: Michael Head
Project Editor: Clare Hubbard
Editor: Lydia Darbyshire

Typeset in Great Britain by
Central Southern Typesetters, Eastbourne
Manufactured in China by
Regent Publishing Services Ltd
Printed in China by Leefung-Asco Printers Ltd

Material in this book previously appeared in
Creative Christmas Crafts, editor Alison Wormleighton,
Creative Nature Crafts, Alison Jenkins with text by Tessa Eveleigh,
Discover Rubber Stamping by Terry McEwan and Jenny Hume,
Giftwrappings for Every Occasion by Gill Dickinson,
Make it with Paper by Paul Jackson and Vivien Frank,
Pop-up Greeting Cards by Mike Palmer,
The Artificial Flower Arranger's Companion by Pat Reeves,
Start a Craft Christmas Crafts by Alison Jenkins,
Start a Craft Greeting Cards by Sharon McSwiney,
Start a Craft Stenciling by Jamie Sapsford and Betsy Skinner

CONTENTS

INTRODUCTION **6**

MATERIALS AND EQUIPMENT **10**

BIRTHDAYS **16**

SPECIAL OCCASIONS **58**

CHRISTMAS AND NEW YEAR **80**

EASTER, HALLOWEEN,
AND HARVEST **128**

GOOD LUCK
AND CONGRATULATIONS **142**

VALENTINE'S DAY **162**

MOTHER'S DAY **178**

INDEX **192**

INTRODUCTION

The cost of shop-bought cards and gift-wrapping paper seems to increase almost daily, and how frustrating it is to spend almost as much on paper and ribbon as on the gift itself, only to be disappointed with the end result. This book contains everything you need to know to create the perfect wrapping every time. Not only does it show how to wrap parcels of every imaginable size and shape, but it also explains how to make and decorate paper. There are instructions for making gift tags and dozens of unusual cards, including cut-outs and pop-ups for every occasion.

There seem to be more and more occasions for exchanging gifts and cards – Christmas, birthdays, Easter, Halloween, weddings, Valentine's Day, Mother's Day . . . the list goes on and on. In the pages that follow you will find a wealth of inspirational ideas and techniques for creating dozens of different looks for presents and greeting cards. Whether you need to wrap a gift for a dedicated gardener (cover the wrapping paper with dried leaves and berries) create a fun gift for a child (make a giant pencil and fill it with novelty pens and pencils) or whether you want to make a card to celebrate a wedding, there is an original idea to delight everyone.

Handmade cards are often kept for far longer than commercially made ones, not simply because they are so much more personal than shop-bought ones and show that you have spent time and trouble thinking about the occasion and the recipient. Handmade cards are often little works of art in their own right, and they may even be kept and framed as an original picture. Many contemporary craft workers and artists produce their own greetings cards, to sell and to give to their own relatives and friends, because they can be a unique form of expression.

Making greetings cards enables you to achieve excellent results in a short space of time and with very few materials. Because the scale is small and the techniques are, usually, simple to master, it is possible to produce something that looks professional without any specific art training. Many of the projects described in this book require nothing more than a few paints, some colored card, a crayon or pen, and your imagination. You can use sponges or your fingers instead of paintbrushes and allow your designs to evolve as you explore the different techniques. Some of the techniques described can be adapted for multiple use, so you can, if you wish, produce many cards at a time. Others are more involved and require the use of several techniques, but the instructions given will enable you to create individual, very special cards.

The emphasis throughout is on using natural and recycled materials whenever possible to create beautiful gift wrappings. Often there is no need to buy expensive ribbons, paper, and gift tags when you can find an amazing range of materials and inspiration all around you – in the garden, on the beach, or among the things you might otherwise throw away.

Keep a box for your collection of gift-wrapping accessories, from old buttons to odds and ends of ribbon and string. Whenever you take a walk along a beach or in a forest, keep an eye out for interesting natural objects, such as shells, driftwood, seaweed, leaves, pine cones, berries, and flowers. Keep old cards and pretty wrapping papers – you can cut out motifs from them for your new designs.

Most of the projects and techniques can be enjoyed by the whole family. Children will love making their own wrapping paper and tags with potato printing, paint spattering, and simple stencils. If you use recycled materials – decorating plain brown paper, for example – these techniques are also inexpensive. If you run out of ideas, simply look through the pages that follow and you are sure to come up with something original.

MATERIALS AND EQUIPMENT

PAINTS AND INKS

Designer gouache, which is available in tubes or small pots, is water-soluble. It gives an even, matt finish, is fast drying, and is easily mixed to create new shades, although a huge range is offered by the manufacturers. It is readily available from art shops and good stationery suppliers.

Ornamental sprays, which include gold and silver metallic spray paints and automobile spray paints, can be bought in hardware stores, art shops, and automobile repair stores. The paint is available in cans. When you use a spray paint, it is a good idea to make a "spray booth" from a large cardboard box. Always use sprays in a well-ventilated room, or, even better, work outside. You may have to practice to avoid applying too much paint at a time.

Block printing ink is water-soluble and is sold in tubes. It is used straight from the tube – there is no need to dilute it with water. It is also possible to obtain oil-based block printing inks, but these take much longer to dry. The inks are available in a range of colors, but black tends to give the best and most consistent results. The ink is available in art shops.

Drawing ink is available in small bottles or jars. It is water-soluble and can be applied with brushes, although you should wash them thoroughly immediately after use, or with steel-nib dipping pens. Various colors are available, including metallic gold and silver. It can be bought from art or craft shops.

Wax crayons and candles are useful resist materials. The crayons intended for children, which are available from art shops and stationery stores, are ideal, because they are inexpensive, non-toxic, and available in a wide range of colors and sizes. White household candles are available from hardware stores.

Glitter can be used to add sparkle to almost any design. Glitter glue (which has glitter in the adhesive solution) or loose glitter can be used. Glitter glue is applied directly to the design. Practice first on a scrap piece of card. It should be the kind of card that you are going to use for your finished item, and also test your paints or crayons as some of the glues will blot and smudge. Loose glitter is applied by putting small amounts of glue on the appropriate parts of the design and shaking the glitter over the image. Work over a large sheet of paper so that surplus glitter can be poured back into the container. Whichever method you use, allow the glue to dry before moving the card or trying to insert it in an envelope.

PENS AND PENCILS

You will find a selection of different pens, pencils, and crayons useful. A fine, permanent black drawing pen, a black, water-soluble marker pen, a selection of ordinary felt- or fiber-tipped pens, and some gold and silver markers are all valuable additions to your equipment. You will also need some pencils, including a general-purpose HB pencil, a softer 4B, for transferring designs, and some inexpensive colored pencils, which are always useful for adding small decorative details.

ADHESIVES

One of the most convenient and tidiest of adhesives is a glue stick, of which there are several proprietary brands. They are all solid blocks of adhesive in a plastic tube, and they are particularly useful for bonding pieces of paper when only a small amount of adhesive is required or when you need to apply adhesive in a small, difficult-to-get-at area. They make it easy to control the amount of glue you apply and are especially suitable for children to use.

Many adhesives are sold in tubes, and they tend to be stronger than the adhesive in glue sticks. They are, therefore, necessary for sticking thicker papers and cards and for attaching non-paper items. Make sure you use them in a well-ventilated room.

A useful all-purpose glue is PVA adhesive, which is a non-toxic, water-based glue. Although it is a milky white, it dries clear, and it is available in plastic bottles and tins from craft shops and hardware stores. Excess glue can be removed by gently rubbing it off the paper with your finger. It can be applied with a brush, but you must wash the brush thoroughly in warm water immediately after use. For large pieces of paper a plastic spatula is useful for giving even coverage. PVA adhesive is also suitable for bonding fabrics, and if you are using fine or delicate fabrics, dilute the adhesive before use.

Double-sided adhesive tape is a useful alternative to glue and is essential for precisely folded parcels. It gives a strong, neat bond, and you can cut off small pieces and place them exactly where they are required. The tape is strong enough to hold card, and will also hold many non-paper items. Also useful are double-sided adhesive pads, which are small foam pads with a strong adhesive on both sides. They can be used for joining most materials, and are useful when you want to create a slightly three-dimensional effect.

A roll of masking tape is always useful to have. It can be easily removed from most surfaces without damaging them, and it is, therefore, invaluable for temporarily securing items, such as stencils, while you work. You can obtain special low-tack tape, which is especially easy to remove. Masking tape is available not only in stationery stores and art shops, but also many hardware shops, where it is often cheaper.

11

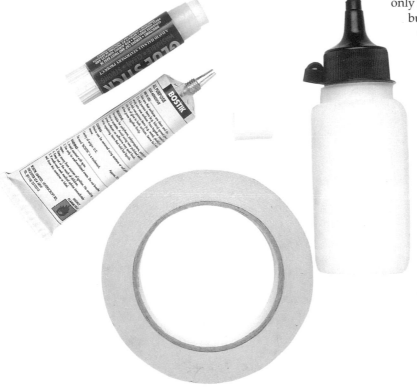

EQUIPMENT

If you are going to use a scalpel or craft knife for cutting out shapes you must protect your working surface. Although a piece of thick cardboard will do, you will find that the surface quickly becomes scored and makes it impossible to cut absolutely neat lines every time. A synthetic cutting mat, made from dense plastic, allows you to cut into it many times without damage. These mats are fairly expensive, but if you are going to use one regularly it will be more than worth the initial outlay. Most of the mats have grids superimposed on the surface, making it easy to position your ruler or set square to get perfect angles and straight lines.

There will be times when scissors are just not maneuverable enough, and you will need to cut out shapes with a craft knife or scalpel. Craft knives, which can also be used for general cutting of card, have snap-off, retractable blades, which are especially useful because you can be sure that you always have a sharp cutting tool. Craft knives in a range of styles are widely available. For safety, always store your craft knife with the blade retracted into the handle. Scalpels are sometimes needed for intricate cutting, and these are available from art shops. Protect the pointed blade with a cork. When you dispose of a scalpel blade or a section of blade from a craft knife, wrap it in a piece of masking tape and then in another piece of paper. Remember that all blades can be dangerous, but scalpel blades are especially sharp.

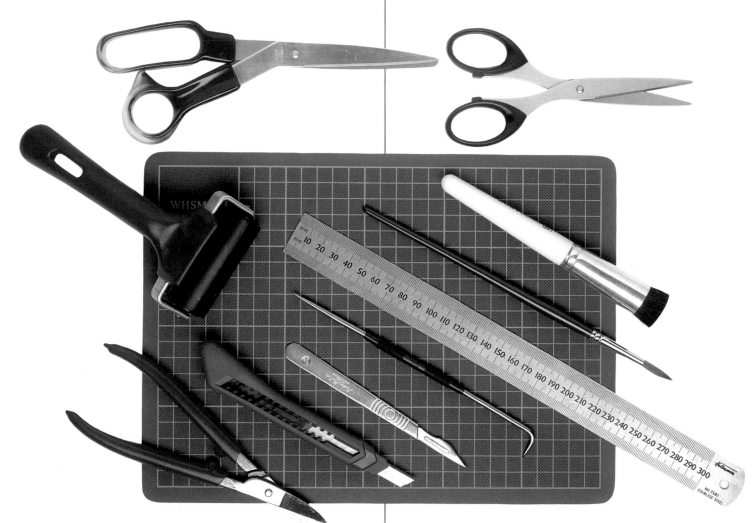

It is worth investing in at least two pairs of good, general-purpose scissors, which should, if you use them only for cutting paper, last for years. A pair of large scissors will be needed for cutting pieces of card, while smaller, pointed scissors are useful for cutting around curves and for snipping out smaller shapes. It is also possible to buy deckle-edged scissors, which will cut a random pattern and which are an easy, quick way of adding a feathered edge to paper and card. Pinking shears can be used to give a zigzag edge to paper and material. If you use fabric for any of the projects, make sure that you keep a special pair of scissors for all your needlework. Nothing blunts sewing scissors more quickly than using them to cut paper.

An ordinary paper punch will come in useful in all kinds of projects, but perhaps even more useful is a leather punch, which can be used to make single holes in card and fabric as well as paper. It has a revolving, star-shaped section that enables you to cut holes in up to six different sizes.

You will find that as well as an ordinary ruler, a metal rule is useful for cutting accurate edges with a craft knife. Always cut away from your body, and make sure that the card or paper to cut is resting on a cutting mat or thick piece of cardboard. A steel ruler will last longer than a wooden or plastic ruler. Some metal rulers have a rubber backing to stop them slipping when you press against them.

If you are going to use metal – perhaps as a stencil or as a

decorative element in a card – you will need a pair of metal- or tin-snips. These are available from specialist jewelry tool suppliers, usually by mail order, or from good hardware stores. If you are not planning to cut metal regularly, you will find that a sharp pair of strong household scissors will do. A metal scriber, used to make designs in metal, will give a good, sharp line, but an old ball-point pen will often do just as well. It is a good idea to wear gloves when you are working with metal – the sharp edges can cause nasty cuts.

You will need several paintbrushes, which come in a bewildering range of qualities and sizes. Sable brushes can be very expensive, although if they are looked after and used only for paints, they will last for years. Synthetic brushes or ones with a mixture of real hair and synthetic materials are suitable for most work. You should aim to have at least one very fine brush, one medium sized one, and one broad, flat brush.

with ink pads, similar to those used in the office, although in a wide range of colors. Pigment inks, which are thick and rather creamy, are slow drying, but they are ideal for good, deep colors. Embossing inks are lightly tinted or colorless. They are slow-drying and are excellent for good embossed results. Embossing powders are available in metallic, transparent, and colored finishes. The powder is a heat-sensitive compound that solidifies when it is exposed to extreme temperatures. The easiest way of applying heat is by means of a hand-held paint stripper, but you can use an iron, an oven plate, or even a hot light bulb. Do not let the heat source come into contact with the embossing powder and do not over-heat the powder or it will look rather dull and unexciting.

Ordinary synthetic household sponges, torn or cut into pieces, can be used to apply paints. Use a separate piece of sponge for each color, and discard them after use.

Stencil brushes are available in a range of sizes and types. They have short, thick handles, and the brushes are cut off flat. You will find them in all good art shops.

Sometimes you will want to use a roller to spread ink evenly over a printing surface. Rollers are available from art shops and some hardware stores. After use, wash immediately in warm water. If you have used an oil-based ink, clean the roller with mineral (white) spirit.

Some of the projects use rubber stamps. When you are choosing your first stamp, look for a pattern or motif that can be used in several ways: craft and art shops stock an increasing range of designs, and some toy stores sell stamps representing characters from children's books, tv programs, and movies. You will find designs ranging from simple, individual letters to intricate patterns. The stamps are used

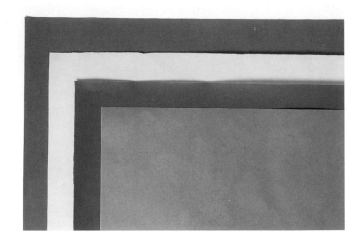

PAPER AND CARD

If you go into any art or craft shop you will find an enormous variety of papers and cards. Collect a range of colors, weights, and textures. Sugar paper, Ingres paper, and cartridge paper are all useful and come in a spectrum of colors. An inexpensive watercolor paper, which is suggested for use in some of the card projects, is useful because it will not break down when it is damp. This kind of paper also often has a slight texture, which can be exploited in your designs. Other useful papers and cards to keep are ordinary brown wrapping paper, tissue paper, foils, thin detail paper, gold and silver card, mounting board, inexpensive cardboard, and any unusually textured or handmade papers that you come across.

When you are preparing to make your own gift wraps and

cards, try to reuse paper whenever you can – tissue paper, brown paper, and even old gift-wrapping paper will all come in useful. Spattering paint onto crumpled tissue paper, for example, is a quick and easy way to create some original wrapping paper.

It is possible to obtain pre-cut card blanks. These are supplied and scored in a variety of sizes, colors, and types of card, and they can be used for many of the cards described. Many of them have pre-cut windows in ovals, hearts, squares, and rectangles, which are very useful. The cards are available in art and craft shops, and an even greater range is available by mail order. Look in the back of almost any craft magazine. However, you can easily cut out your own cards from a medium weight card, which gives you flexibility with both size and color. Choose a card that is heavy enough to stand upright but is not so thick that it will not fold neatly.

BIRTHDAYS

In this section are all kinds of ideas for decorating gifts of all shapes and sizes in unusual and attractive ways. There are also dozens of ideas for cards and gift tags. Many of these ideas can be used – with different materials, colors, and finishes – for other occasions than birthdays, and you will find suggestions in other sections of this book that can easily be translated into pretty, unusual, and original ideas for birthdays. There are several pop-up cards in this section. Few of them require any great degree of artistic skill, but they do require a little care and precision.

In addition to guidelines for creating the perfectly wrapped square or rectangular parcel every time, there are also some ingenious ideas for those gifts that sometimes refuse to be wrapped up neatly – bottles are always difficult, and many cosmetics come in odd shapes. Bags are easy to make and can look extremely decorative, and they have the advantage that you can make them fit any size or shape. Decorate them with handmade tags or add an unusual handle.

WRAPPING A BOX

Although a box is an easy shape to wrap, it's still important that the gift looks good.

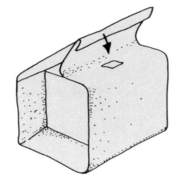

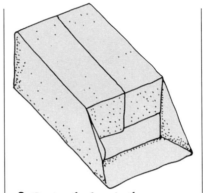

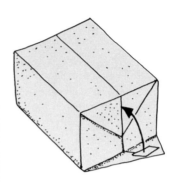

18

1. Cut the paper to fit the box. You will need an overlap at the top of about 4in and two-thirds the box height at the sides. Fold down the top by ⅜in from the edge. Center fold on the box and hold down with double-sided adhesive tape.

2. Center the box in the paper and press the folded edge against the box. Crease the side folds before pushing them in.

3. Fold up the triangular fold and fix with double-sided tape. Repeat at the other end of the box.

The delicate tissue papers have been decorated with relief fabric paints, which are easy to draw with and can be used straight from the tube. These papers have a seashore theme – shells and fish – but the technique can be used for abstract designs as well as pictorial ones.

TURN TURTLE

The technique used to make this appealing card requires very little equipment, but once you have made the "master" design you can make as many versions of it as you wish, using different colored wax crayons and different mounting card to create cards suitable for dozens of occasions. This motif was inspired by Australian Aboriginal designs, but the same method could be used for all kinds of patterns.

YOU WILL NEED

Tracing paper
Pencils (medium hard and very soft)
2 pieces white cartridge or sugar paper, 11½ × 8¼in
Scissors or craft knife
Clear, all-purpose adhesive or glue stick
Detail paper
Wax crayons: purple, blue
Maroon card, about 9¼ × 6¼in

Enlarge by 30% on a photocopier to trace at full size

1. Place some tracing paper over the design and draw it with a medium hard pencil. Turn over the design and rub over the whole area with a soft (4B) pencil. Place the tracing paper, right side up, over the cartridge paper and go over the lines with a medium hard pencil so that the lines of the design are transferred to the paper.

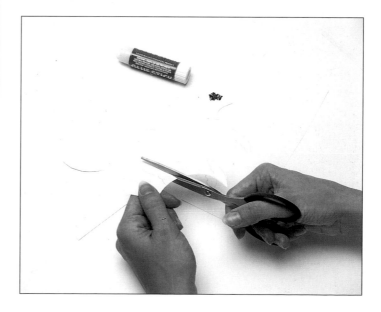

2. Use sharp, pointed scissors or a craft knife to cut out the sections of the motifs.

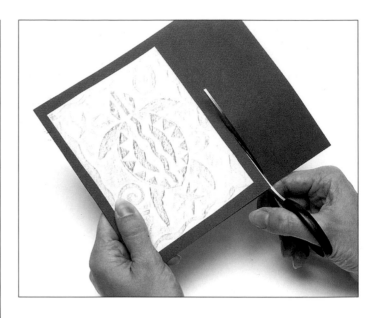

3. Paste the cut-out shapes of the design onto a clean sheet of paper, including all the additional decorative features such as borders, stars, and swirls. Leave until the glue is dry.

5. Trim the detail paper to size if necessary, and glue it to a larger piece of card of a contrasting color. Fold this to form a greeting card and trim to size.

4. Place some thin detail paper over the design and use a wax crayon to rub over the surface. Make sure that the detail paper is perfectly smooth and clean, and rub carefully over the surface in all directions to get an even cover. Use different colors for the different parts of the design.

SUN AND MOON PRINTED CARD

Mono-printing is an easy-to-master technique, and you can use it to create one-off prints. A sun and moon motif was used for this card, which would be suitable for a birthday card, but this is one of the techniques that can be used for all kinds of patterns and designs. Linear designs are usually most successful, but you can add tone by applying pressure with your fingers to specific areas. The exciting thing about it is that, until you peel back the paper, you cannot tell exactly how the print is going to turn out.

YOU WILL NEED

Black block printing ink	Pencil
Sheet of glass, about	Clear, all-purpose adhesive
11½ × 8¼in	Silver card
2½in ink roller	Maroon card, 8 × 6in
White sugar paper, about	Fine silver marker pen
6¼ × 4¼in	

Enlarge by 30% on a photocopier to trace at full size

2. Carefully place a piece of paper on the inked glass and use a sharp pencil to draw the design. The print will be the reverse of what you draw, and you can experiment with the pressure you apply to the pencil to give lighter and darker lines.

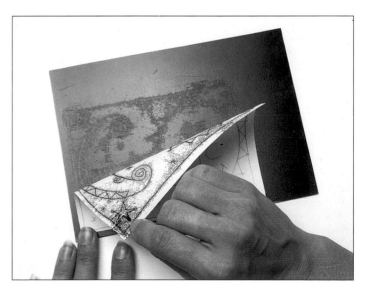

3. When the design is complete, carefully peel back the paper to reveal the print. Leave to dry. If you have used a water-soluble ink, this will take 20–30 minutes; if you have used an oil-based ink, leave for at least 2 hours.

1. Place a small amount of ink on the glass and use the roller to spread it evenly over the surface. Begin with a little ink, then gradually add more.

4. When the print is dry, glue it to a background of silver card, and trim to size, leaving a border of about ½in all round.

5. If you wish, add further decoration by "scoring" patterns in the surface of the silver card with a sharp pencil.

6. Firmly glue the mounted print to the larger, folded card blank. If you use a strongly contrasting color – like the maroon shown here – add a decorative border around the card with a fine silver marker pen.

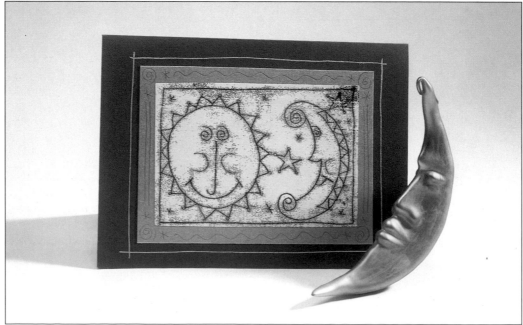

PAINT STENCILS

The stencil used for this card is acetate rather than cardboard. Not only do acetate stencils last longer than those made of cardboard so you can use them time after time, but it is possible to create more complex designs with finer details. The motif used here – a crocodile – was, like the turtle card (see page 19), inspired by the art of the Australian Aborigines. The earthy colors represent the natural pigments used by native Australians, but other shades would look good. Stencil paints are available from most art shops, but they can be rather expensive. Gouache or latex paint works just as well.

YOU WILL NEED

Acetate, 11½ × 8¼in
Fine felt-tipped pen
Scalpel or craft knife
Masking tape
Ingres paper: orange and
    dark brown, 7¾ × 3½in
Gouache paint: red, orange
Palette or saucer

Stencil brush
Colored pencils: red,
    orange, brown, yellow
Paintbrush (no. 7)
Clear, all-purpose adhesive
    or glue stick
Scissors
Cream card, 7¾ × 7½in

2. Use masking tape to hold the acetate stencil over the chosen paper to prevent it from slipping. Apply paint over the whole of the stencil with a stencil brush.

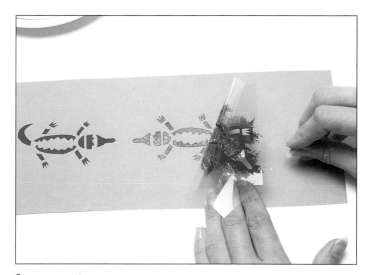

3. Remove the masking tape and carefully peel back the stencil, leaving a print of the design. Repeat the process as many times as you wish. Leave the paint to dry for 20–30 minutes.

1. Trace the design onto a piece of acetate with a fine pen and use a scalpel or craft knife to remove the dark sections of the motif. Remove any ink that remains on the surface of the acetate with a damp tissue.

4. Carefully tear the paper to size and use colored pencils to complete the design.

6. When the paint is dry, stick it to a background of a contrasting color. Cut it to size, leaving a narrow border of the contrasting color showing around the edge.

5. Highlight the torn edges of the paper and create a border by adding a small amount of paint to the edges with a fine paintbrush.

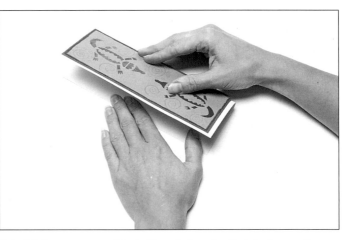

7. Fold the cream card in half and glue the finished stencil to the front of the larger piece of card.

METAL MAGIC

Rather than taking all your empty aluminum drink cans to the recycling tip, try this unique method of decorating a greeting card. Linear or punched patterns can be easily created in the soft aluminum, giving an embossed effect. It is the perfect technique for all kinds of decorations. A simple bird motif was used in this project, which was inspired by American folk art. You may want to wear gloves when you are cutting the metal because the edges are quite sharp.

YOU WILL NEED

Empty aluminum can
Metal scriber
Metal snips
Tracing paper
Fine, black felt-tipped pen
Fine wire wool
Pencil and ruler

Dark blue mounting card,
   3½ × 3in
Craft knife
White card, 8 × 6in
Double-sided adhesive
   tape
Fine silver marker pen

1. Carefully pierce the can with a scriber to make a hole. Insert the snips into the hole and cut off the top of the can.

2. Cut down the side of the can and remove the base. Once the metal is opened out, trim off any uneven edges and cut off a section of metal to work with.

3. Transfer the image of the bird to the reverse (patterned) side of the metal. Use a felt-tipped pen rather than a ball-point pen so that you do not mark the metal. Arrange the motif so that there is at least ½in all round. Go over the lines of the design with a scriber.

26

4. When you have completed scribing gently rub over the surface of the metal with wire wool and trim it to size if necessary. Place the metal on a piece of mounting card and draw a line around it. The card will form the mount for the metal.

5. Measure, then draw a border on the mounting board. Draw a third line, at least ¼in inside the first, so that the mount will hold the metal in place.

6. Cut along the outside line on the cardboard, and then cut out the central window of the blue card.

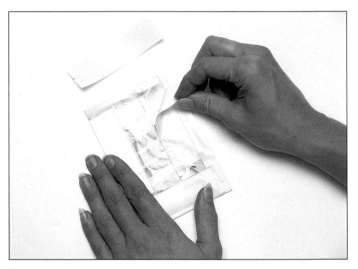

7. Use double-sided tape to stick the metal to the front of the white card. Tape is better than adhesive because the metal has a springy quality that makes it difficult for glue to adhere to the surface.

8. Use more tape to stick the blue frame to the front of the card so that the motif is centered in the window. If you wish, add small decorative dots with a silver pen.

INVITATIONS AND TAKE-HOME BAGS

This bright and festive invitation would be suitable for almost any occasion, but the matching "take-home" bags are ideal for a children's party, when the guests have little presents to take home with them. The motif and decorations are created with simple rubber stamps, and although the pigment ink pad looks rather intimidating, it is easy to use and creates wonderful effects. The materials listed below are sufficient for one card and one bag.

YOU WILL NEED

2 rectangles cream card, each about 5 × 3in
Rubber stamps: star burst, crown, frame
Symphonic pigment ink pad
Crystal embossing powder
Heat source
Deckle-edged scissors
Green card, 8 × 6in
Red paper, 5½ × 3½in
Clear, all-purpose adhesive
Sharp, pointed scissors or craft knife
Colored paper bag
Silver pigment pad
Cosmetic sponge
Self-adhesive pads or double-sided adhesive tape
Silver felt-tipped pen

1. Place one of the rectangles of cream card on a piece of scrap paper and, using the blue and green section of the ink pad and the star burst stamp, print around the edge of the paper so about half the image appears.

2. Using the yellow and red portion of the ink pad, print the crown in the center of the cream card. Before the paint is dry, shake some crystal embossing powder on the surface. Apply heat (a hand-held paint stripper is ideal), following the manufacturer's instructions.

3. Trim the edge of the cream card with deckle-edged scissors or tear it carefully against a metal ruler.

4. Score and fold the green card and stick the red paper to the front of it. Finish by positioning the cream card on the red paper and sticking it in place.

5. Make the bag by using the yellow and red section of the ink pad, ink the crown and print it in the center of the other rectangle of cream card.

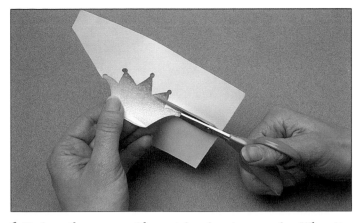

6. Emboss the crown with crystal embossing powder. When it is cool and perfectly dry, carefully cut out the crown with sharp scissors or a craft knife and put it to one side.

8. Use a piece of cosmetic sponge to make a cloud of silver ink below the frame.

7. Ink the frame stamp with silver ink and print the image on the top section of the bag.

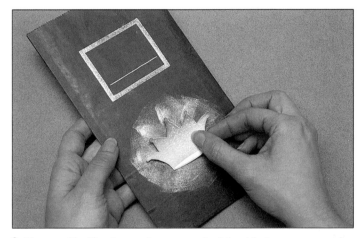

9. Use a self-adhesive pad or some double-sided tape to attach the crown to the bag in the center of the silver cloud. Add the recipient's name with a silver felt-tipped pen.

PENCIL PACKAGING

A large colored paper pencil is a novel way to wrap a gift. Fill the pencil with novelty items, stationery, or with sweets. If the pencil is large enough, use it for a T-shirt, scarf, or pair of gloves. Fill the end of the pencil with crumpled tissue paper and make a pencil gift tag in a contrasting color.

YOU WILL NEED

Medium weight paper:
   white, yellow, blue
Tracing paper
Ruler
Scalpel
Double-sided adhesive
   tape or clear, all-
   purpose adhesive

30

1. Cut out a rectangle of yellow paper measuring 11 × 10in. Use the template (ABOVE) to cut out the point of the pencil from pieces of yellow and white paper.

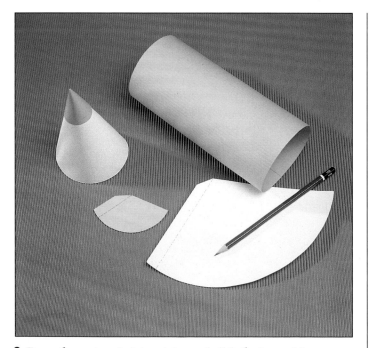

2. Form the rectangle into a tube and stick the long sides together. Form the yellow and white points into cones, making sure that they fit inside the end of the tube. Stick the yellow cone over the white cone.

3. Make a contrasting pencil tag and thread through some plastic thread. Push the top of the pencil into the tube and hold it in place with adhesive tape.

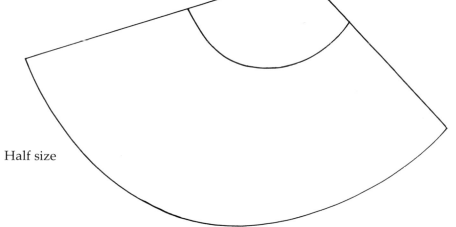

Half size

TWIST-OUT CARDS

This is an ingenious way of creating three-dimensional cards. Use thin card – paper is too weak, and thick card is too cumbersome to bend easily. The basic method is explained here, and the technique can be easily adapted to all kinds of shapes, geometric and representational.

YOU WILL NEED

Card
Scalpel or craft knife
Scissors
Pencil and ruler

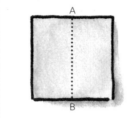

1. Draw a line (AB) down the center of a piece of card.

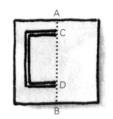

2. Use a blade to incise line C to D so that the incision starts and ends on AB. Note that AC is shorter than DB.

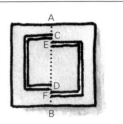

3. Next, incise line E to F so that the incision starts and ends on line AB. Note that E is below C and F is below D.

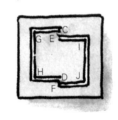

4. Pull edge GH towards you and push IJ away from you, forming short creases between CE and DF.

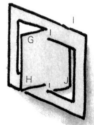

5. The center of the card will twist out from its frame.

BELOW: Twist-outs make highly individual greeting cards. The words and shapes can be altered to suit every occasion.

QUILLED GIFT TAGS

The technique of quilling or paper filigree involves using rolled strips of paper to form shapes, which can be glued together and stuck to a base card to make patterns. The designs can be used in various ways, but they are especially appropriate for gift tags and small cards. The strips should be about ⅛in wide, and the length can vary. Some stationery shops sell pre-cut strips, and these are worth looking out for because cutting them by hand is extremely laborious, especially if you are planning a fairly ambitious project.

Use a cocktail stick, matchstick, or a piece of dowel with a split in the end. Place one end of the strip in the split and turn it slowly and evenly so that the strip remains level. When the paper is completely rolled, squeeze it lightly to make a tight curve before removing the stick.

You can plan patterns in advance or build them up as you go along. It is best to work on a piece of waxed paper so that you can move the designs around as your work progresses. If you are making a decoration for a card and have a good idea of the scheme, glue the center of the shape and place each part of the design carefully in position. A second cocktail stick or a pair of tweezers are useful for controlling the coils. Finished designs can be sprayed with paint or varnish.

Plain gift tags can be decorated using quilling. Use the little coils of paper to create some unusual shapes and patterns.

WHAT A CRACKER!

Most pop-up cards open with a single crease, but here, to mimic the movement of an exploding cracker, two creases are needed. To hold the design tight shut during transit, a lock must be constructed across the central opening. Note how the four pop-up elements fly off two small rectangular tabs cut from the backing sheet and off two triangles glued to it. The triangles can be cut from the backing sheet, but this will weaken the card. The grid is drawn to a scale of 1:2.

YOU WILL NEED

Backing sheet (thin red glossy card), 12 × 8in
Adhesive tape
Blue and yellow glossy card (for letters),

10 × 4in in total
Blue foil on white card (for cracker), about 8 × 6in
Scissors

Craft knife or scalpel
Clear, all-purpose adhesive

KEY

— cut along this line
— suggested artwork
— mountain crease
— valley crease
▢ glue here (sometimes on the underside)

34

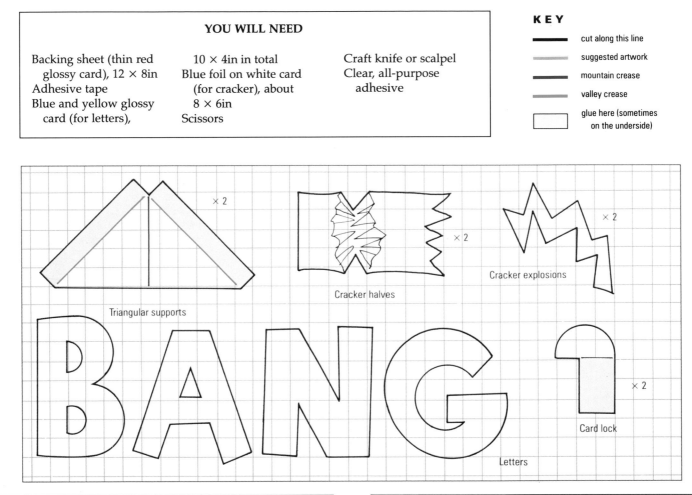

Triangular supports

× 2

Cracker halves

× 2

Cracker explosions

× 2

BANG

Card lock

× 2

Letters

1. Use the template (ABOVE) to cut out the pieces. Incise small square tabs as shown, one on each crease of the backing sheet. Glue the triangular supports flat against the creases.

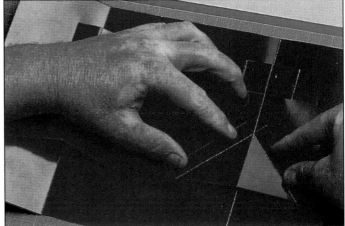

2. Make sure that the creases on the support align accurately with the creases on the triangles.

3. Glue the letters B and A to the left-hand support.

4. Glue N and G to the other support.

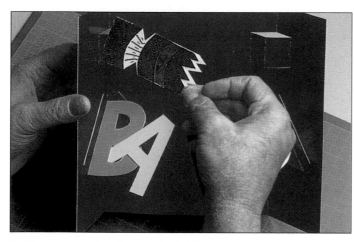

5. Glue one cracker half to the left-hand square tab.

6. Similarly, glue the other half to the right-hand tab. Add the explosions.

7. Close the card and add the two halves of the lock, intertwining them. When they are carefully aligned, the lock halves will hold the card tightly shut.

FOR THE UNDER-10s

This design uses a single piece of card and a cut-away technique to make part of the pop-up – the top half of the number – stand freely. When you are making the card, measure the distances carefully so that the number is well proportioned and well positioned. Working out the geometry of a single-piece pop-up card can be difficult. The simple step shape used here, with the top half of the number lifted from the background, can be adapted for other numbers or letters or even words and objects. The grid is drawn to a scale of 1:2½.

YOU WILL NEED

Medium weight blue
  paper, 12¾ × 6in
Scissors or scalpel
Yellow self-adhesive dots
Felt-tipped pens

KEY

———— cut along this line

———— suggested artwork

———— mountain crease

———— valley crease

———— these measurements
      are the same

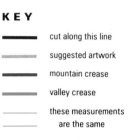

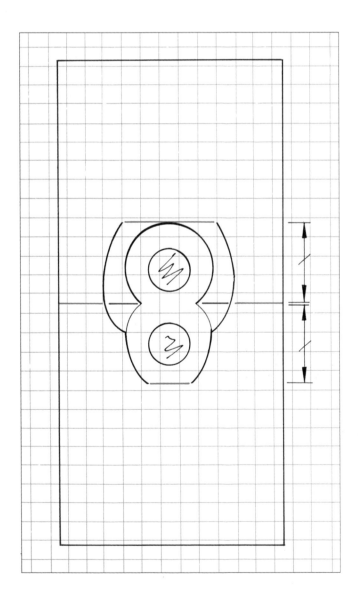

1. Cut along the solid lines shown on the template (LEFT).

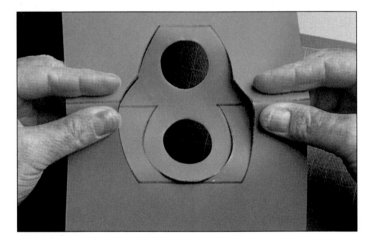

2. Fold the two ends of the central crease.

3. Fold the bottom crease.

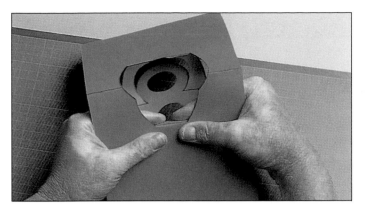

4. Fold along the top crease and turn the card over.

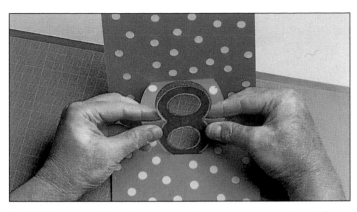

5. Fold the remaining short, central creases at each side of the number.

6. This is the completed pop-up shape, which will fold flat.

LIGHT THE CANDLE

One-piece pop-up cards are always satisfying to make because you can see a three-dimensional shape emerge as if by magic from what was a flat piece of card. The geometry, though, can be a little mystifying. The key is to measure the placement of all the creases carefully and to understand which distances are equal to other distances. For best results, before making a finished card, make a rough card so that you can check that you understand which measurements must be equal. The grid is drawn to a scale of 1:2½.

KEY

——— cut along this line

——— suggested artwork

——— mountain crease

——— valley crease

——— these measurements
           are the same

YOU WILL NEED

Thin cream-colored card,
    13½ × 6in
Ruler
Scalpel
Felt-tipped pens or
    crayons

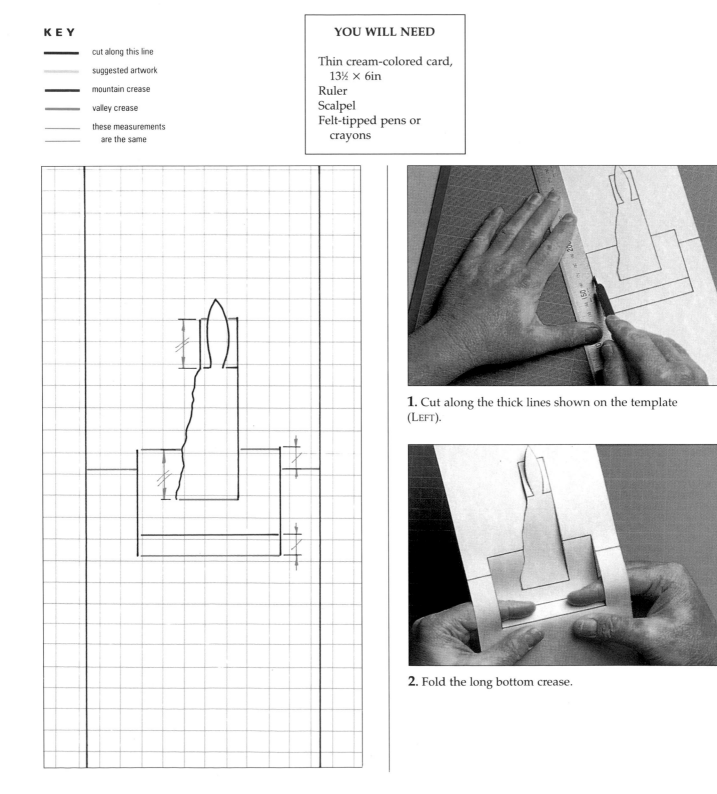

1. Cut along the thick lines shown on the template (LEFT).

2. Fold the long bottom crease.

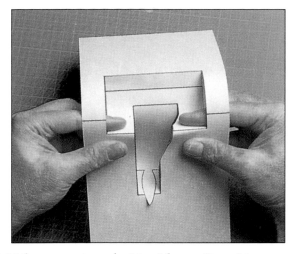

3. Fold the creases to each side of the candle and turn over the card carefully.

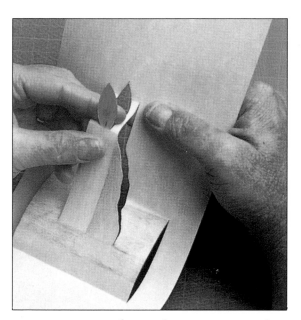

4. Fold the creases around the flame.

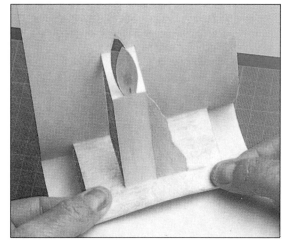

5. Fold the front edge of the step to complete the card.

6. The completed pop-up card. Careful measuring and creasing will permit the candle to fold flat.

CLASHING COLORS

Bright and jazzy giftwrap appeals to adults and children alike. Wrapping ordinary boxes in wonderfully colored papers is a simple way of creating fun gift wrapping.
Choose a paint that contrasts with the paper. Make it quite runny, dip in an old toothbrush and flick on to the paper. Decorate with paper ribbon and sweets.
Spatter a box with a clashing color of paint and make a matching tag. Wrap with paper ribbon and add some marzipan vegetables threaded on to a wooden skewer.

40

STAMPED GIFT TAGS

These simple little tags are easy to make but are a perfect way of adding a personal touch to a gift. Mulberry paper is like tissue paper, but it has a fibrous texture. It can be used to print on and emboss with powder, and it is ideal for all kinds of decorative uses. When it is torn, the edges feather prettily.

YOU WILL NEED

Maple leaf stamp
Ink pad in shades of
   green
Self-adhesive note pad
Sharp, pointed scissors
Cream paper, 3 × 1½in
Dark green mulberry
   paper

Deckle-edged scissors
Clear, all-purpose
   adhesive
Ready-made gift tag blank
   or cream card, scored
   and folded

41

3. When the ink on the printed leaf is dry, place the mask over it. Print a second leaf, to the right of the first one, using the medium shade of green. Clean the stamp.

1. Make a mask by stamping the maple leaf onto a sheet of the note pad – make sure that the image is positioned close to the sticky portion of the pad. Carefully cut out the image and put it to one side.

4. Still with the mask in place over the first leaf, ink the stamp with the light shade of green and print a third leaf, this time to the left of the first one. When the ink is dry, carefully remove the mask.

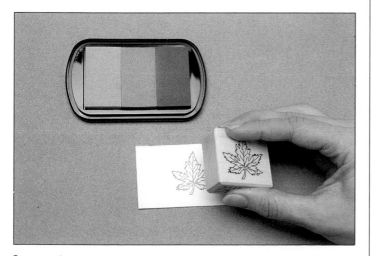

2. Print the leaf in the darkest shade of green on the cream paper. Clean the stamp by pressing it alternately on a damp paper towel and a dry paper towel.

5. Tear or use deckle-edged scissors to cut a piece of the mulberry paper so that it is about ¼in less all round than the gift tag blank.

6. Glue the mulberry paper to the front of the gift tag.

7. Carefully cut out the printed leaves and glue them to the center of the mulberry paper.

STENCIL GIFT TAGS

These little gift tags are simple to make, and they are an ideal project to introduce children to the art of stenciling. A white heart on red paper and a yellow star on green were used, but the colors can be changed to match the wrapping paper. The steps below describe how to make and use a simple stencil.

YOU WILL NEED

Colored paper, 4 × 3in
Hole punch
Tracing paper
Acetate
Scalpel or craft knife
Stencil or acrylic paint
Saucer
Stencil brush
Curling ribbon

2. Practice by putting a small amount of red paint in a saucer or palette. Dip the brush into the paint and then rub off the excess on a paper towel so that the brush is almost dry.

1. Fold the paper in half lengthways and punch a hole in the top left-hand corner, leaving sufficient room for the design. Trace the motif of your choice, lay a piece of acetate on the tracing, and use a craft knife or scalpel to cut out the shape.

3. Place the stencil over a piece of scrap paper and hold it firmly in place with one hand. Hold the stencil brush upright and press it through the stencil cut-out, moving it with a circular motion around the inside edge of the stencil. Continue to build up color by moving the brush around the edges, but try not to let the color build up in the center of the cut-out.

4. If your brush is too wet with paint, it may result in a flat, filled-in stencil shape that bleeds around the edges (as in the top heart). The drier the brush, the better, although if it is too dry the image will be too faint (center heart). The heart at the bottom, with the shaded edges and light center area is ideal.

5. When you are confident, use the technique on the card, building up the color in a circular motion around the edge of the cut-out. Finally, twirl a length of ribbon and thread it through the hole.

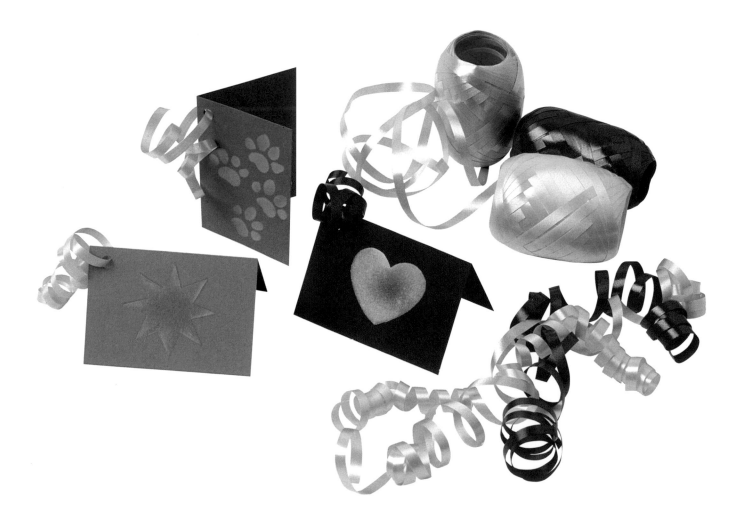

BASIC BOX

When you are drawing a plan for a basic box, work out the dimensions and, whatever the size, make sure that all the angles are 90 degrees (see Fig 1). The larger the box, the thicker the card should be. The number of flaps should equal the number of edges, and all flaps should be at least ½in deep, although if you are making a very large box, you might want to make the flaps 1in or more.

YOU WILL NEED

Thin card
Pencil and ruler
Craft knife or scalpel
Scissors
Bone folder
Pair of compasses
Protractor and/or set
  square
Clear, all-purpose
  adhesive
Double-sided adhesive
  tape

1. Use a sharp craft knife to cut out the shape. Always cut away from your work so that you do not accidentally cut into the box side.

2. Check the fit of the box, then glue the sides together.

3. Glue the base in position.

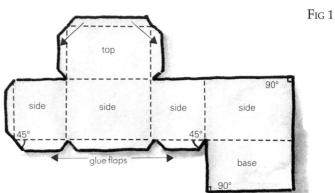

Fɪɢ 1

45

Bᴇʟᴏw: Card can be simply decorated in dozens of ways, including collage, stenciling, and marbling, and then made into boxes to hold all manner of things. Alternatively, use plain card, and add colorful ribbons, bows, and tags, or cover plain card with shop-bought gift-wrap.

HANDMADE PAPER

Each handmade sheet of paper is unique, and it can be used to make unusual wrapping paper, boxes, cards, and envelopes. Handmade paper incorporating flowers and leaves is surprisingly easy to make. Lavender or thyme will give it an aromatic quality, and petals, ferns, and grasses can be added to give color and texture. Before you begin, you need to make a mold and deckle. The mold is a rectangular frame of wood with a fine mesh stretched across it. The deckle is an identical frame without the mesh that sits on top of the mesh side of the mold. You can buy them, but if you want to make your own, see step 1 below.

<table>
<tr><td colspan="2" align="center">YOU WILL NEED</td></tr>
<tr><td>6ft × ¾in wood</td><td>Thin, absorbent kitchen</td></tr>
<tr><td>Saw</td><td>   cloths</td></tr>
<tr><td>Waterproof adhesive</td><td>Sheets of waste paper, such</td></tr>
<tr><td>Nails</td><td>   as newspaper, photocopy</td></tr>
<tr><td>Nylon curtain mesh,</td><td>   paper, old envelopes,</td></tr>
<tr><td>   12 × 12in</td><td>   and so on</td></tr>
<tr><td>Staple gun</td><td>Electric blender</td></tr>
<tr><td>2 pieces of plywood, each</td><td>Flower petals, lavender,</td></tr>
<tr><td>   10 × 12in</td><td>   ferns, herbs, grasses, and</td></tr>
<tr><td>Shallow plastic tray</td><td>   so on</td></tr>
<tr><td>3 large sheets of newspaper</td><td>Plastic dish-washing bowl</td></tr>
</table>

1. Cut the 6ft × ¾in wood into four pieces, each 10in long, and four pieces, each 8in long. Glue the pieces together to form two identical rectangles, butting the corners neatly together. When the glue is dry, nail the pieces together. Stretch the nylon mesh over one of the frames, using a staple gun to hold it taut. Trim away any excess fabric.

2. Make a couching mound to ease the transfer of the layers of paper pulp from the mold to the couching cloths. Lay a plywood rectangle in the shallow tray. Fold the newspaper into various sizes and place them on top of the plywood. Cover with a kitchen cloth and moisten with water.

3. Half fill the blender jug with water. Tear the waste paper into small pieces, about 1 x 1in, and add about two handfuls to the blender jug. Blend for a 10–20 second burst, add the plant materials, and blend for a further 5 seconds. Pour four or five jugs of pulp into the dish-washing bowl and top up with water until the bowl is about half full.

4. Place the wooden deckle on top of the mesh side of the mold, holding both together along the shorter sides. Insert them into the pulp at an angle of about 45 degrees. Draw both up through the pulp so that the mold and deckle are horizontal.

5. Lift the mold and deckle from the water, a layer of paper pulp will have been deposited on the mesh. Hold it over the bowl for a second or two to allow the water to drain away, then remove the deckle, and place the pulp-covered mesh side of the mold on the couching mound.

6. Lift the mold, leaving the pulp layer on the mound. Cover it with another kitchen cloth, and repeat the whole process again. Build up 8–10 layers, then place the other plywood rectangle on top. Squeeze the plywood pieces together to remove excess water. Carefully peel off the kitchen cloths with the pulp layers still attached, and leave them in a warm, dry place to dry completely. The paper sheets can then be removed from the cloths.

ENVELOPES

It is quite simple to make your own envelopes, and when you have taken the trouble to make a card, it seems a shame to spoil the effect by either not finding an envelope that fits or using one that does not match. A natural colored envelope was used here, and decorated simply with a few swirls, but the decoration can be as complicated or as restrained as you want.

YOU WILL NEED

Sheet of paper to match
   card, about 16½ ×
   11¾in
Pencil
Ruler
Scissors
Glue stick

3. Measure from the center point (where the diagonals bisect) to the edge of the top and the edge of the bottom sections. Add this measurement, plus ½in for the overlap, and make a mark. Draw lines from the corners to these marks to form the flaps of the envelope.

1. Place the card for which you are making the envelope on the chosen paper. Measure around the card, allowing a border of ¼in on all sides. Draw in the lines.

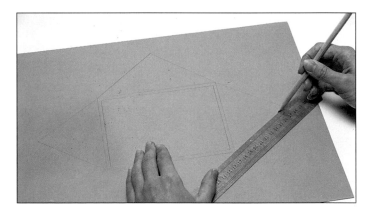

4. Repeat the process for the side flaps, but do not add the extra ½in.

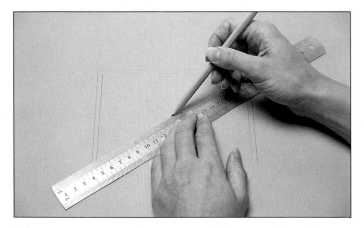

2. Mark the center of your drawing with a cross, drawn by measuring in from the corners.

5. Cut out the finished shape then fold in the flaps at the sides to form an envelope.

6. Apply a small amount of glue to the edges of the bottom of the envelope. Fold it over and stick it down over the side flaps.

7. The envelope can then be decorated with a gold pen, as shown. Alternatively, you can use cork stamps, stencils or whatever you wish to complement the card.

CARDS FROM NATURE

A simple method of producing unique greeting cards is to collect feathers, leaves, seed pods, or dried flowers and mount them onto textured, natural-colored papers. Handmade papers are also available, many of which would complement the natural objects used.

YOU WILL NEED

A feather; chicken or duck feathers are very suitable
Sugar paper in 2 colors; pale beige and pink, 8¼ x 11½in
Natural color blank card, 6 x 8in

Scissors
Craft knife
Masking tape
Cutting mat

50

3. Slide the shaft of the feather through the slits until the feather lies in the desired position on the paper.

1. Select your feather and its background paper. Carefully tear the paper to the correct size. A torn edge will give a more interesting effect.

4. Turn over the paper and keeping the feather in position put a piece of tape over the openings and the feather shaft to secure the feather in place. If decorating with dried leaves, seed pods etc, mount them using PVA glue and leave to dry for 30–40 minutes.

2. Place the backing paper on the cutting mat and with a craft knife, make two slits in the paper.

5. To further decorate the card, select a complementary colored paper for a background. Crumple this sheet of paper in your hands.

6. Flatten out the paper, then tear it to size. Apply glue, then stick this to a larger folded, contrasting card.

7. To complete the greeting card, glue the paper holding the feather onto the middle of the crumpled effect background.

SIMPLE BAG

Bags like this are easy to make, and once you have mastered the technique they can be used in all kinds of ways. Small bags can be made with ordinary gift-wrapping paper, although if you want to make a larger bag you will need to use thicker, stronger paper. You can, for example, use ordinary brown wrapping paper and decorate it before assembling the bag. Remember that all the angles must be perfect right angles so that the bag will stand square and the bottom flaps should be about ½in less than the width of the sides. If you are using thick paper or card, score the fold lines to give crisp, neat creases.

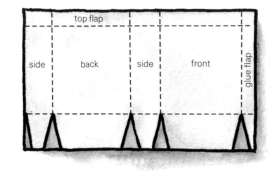

1. It is easiest to work on the wrong side of the paper. Decide on the size of the bag and draw the plan. Cut out the shape and remove the shaded areas. Score the dotted lines lightly, and fold and unfold them.

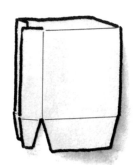

2. Glue down the top flap, which adds strength and looks neater. Next glue the front flap to the side.

3. Finally, glue the bottom flaps to each other – the side flaps to the back flap and the front flap on top of the side flaps.

STRONG PAPER BAG

If you are going to make a bag to contain a heavy gift, such as a bottle, glue a piece of card inside the base of the bag. To strengthen the top, add an extra strip of paper under the top flap. The basic plan is the same as for a simple bag, except that the measurements for all sides should be identical and should be the diameter of the bottle, plus ¼in. The height of the bag should be 2½in more than the height of the bottle so that the top edges can be drawn together.

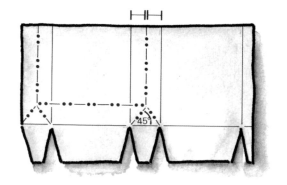

1. It is possible to fold the bag flat by scoring lines in addition to the ones on the basic plan. Practice with some scrap paper – it is not as complicated as it looks.

2. When you are making a large bag, add a strong handle by cutting a piece of plain, lightweight card the width of the bag and at least 3in deep. Cut the hand shape out of the center of the card and mark this hole on the bag plan. Cut these holes out of the paper on the bag and top flap, and glue the card stiffener in position before proceeding as for the basic bag.

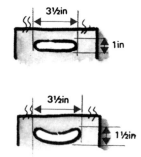

*RIGHT: You can buy chiles
ready dried or you can dry
them yourself. Their brilliant
red color looks wonderful on
gold boxes and bags.*

*BELOW: The strong bag can be
made to fit bottles or smaller,
lighter objects such as scarves
or gloves. Score the lines before
folding to give neat edges.*

GIFT BAGS

These charming little country-look bags take the idea of using bags for awkwardly shaped gifts a stage further — they are perfect for even the most bizarre shapes. Enlarge the size of the template on a photocopier if you want to make a larger bag.

YOU WILL NEED

Tracing paper
White card for template
Ruler and pencil
Check cotton fabric
Paper or card with a
 textured surface
Knife
Scissors
PVA adhesive

Paintbrush
Double-sided adhesive
 tape
Leather punch
Fine string
Small buttons with two
 holes
Thin colored card

2. To make the fabric-covered bag, cut a piece of cloth about 1in larger all round than the template. Glue the card shape to the fabric, carefully smoothing out any wrinkles and bubbles. Trim the fabric close to the card, leaving 1in excess at the upper edge. Crease at the fold positions again.

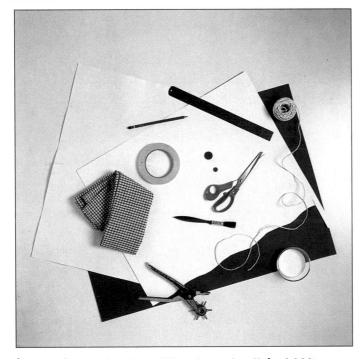

1. Trace the template (page 56) and transfer all the fold lines accurately. The template shows both sizes. For the bag made of card, cut out a box shape in colored or textured card. For the fabric-covered bag, use thin white card. Score along all dotted lines.

3. Use double-sided tape to hold the tab to the side edge.

4. Fold in the flaps at the lower edge to form the bottom of the bag. Hold the flaps in place with double-sided tape.

5. If you are making the fabric-covered bag, apply a strip of double-sided tape to the inside of the top edge. Turn the fabric down neatly all round.

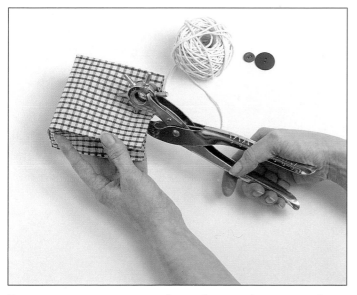

6. Make a fastening by using the leather punch to pierce a hole in the center of the bag, about ¾in down from the top edge.

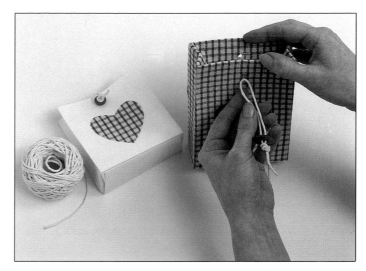

7. Cut a piece of string about 10in long for each bag. Fold the string in half, then thread the ends through the holes in the button and tie a knot. Next, thread the loop end through the punched holes at the top of the bag, then bring the loop around the button at the front. This makes a pretty and secure fastening.

8. To make the fish gift tag, trace the template (page 56). Cut one shape from thin, colored card. Score and fold it along the dotted line. Pierce a small hole at the head end, using a paper punch. Glue on a small button for the eye. Knot a short length of string and tie up the bag with a neat bow.

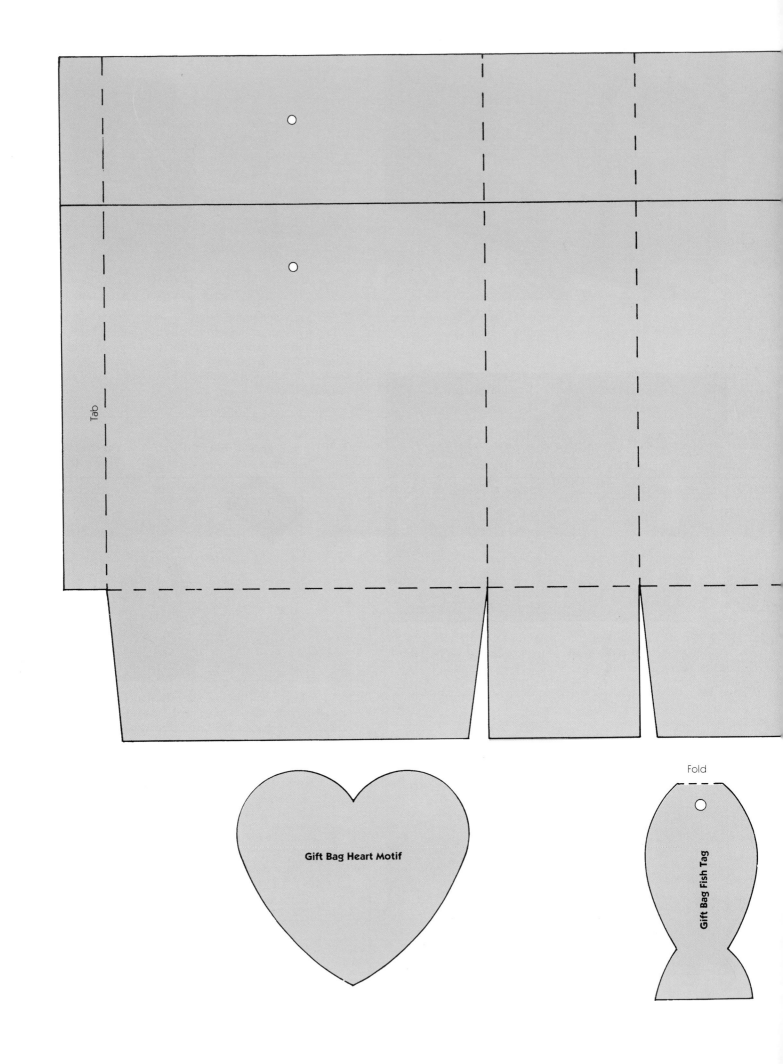

Tab

Gift Bag Heart Motif

Fold

Gift Bag Fish Tag

Large Bag

○

Small Bag

○

Gift Bags

Cut along solid lines
Score and fold along dotted lines

Side Edge

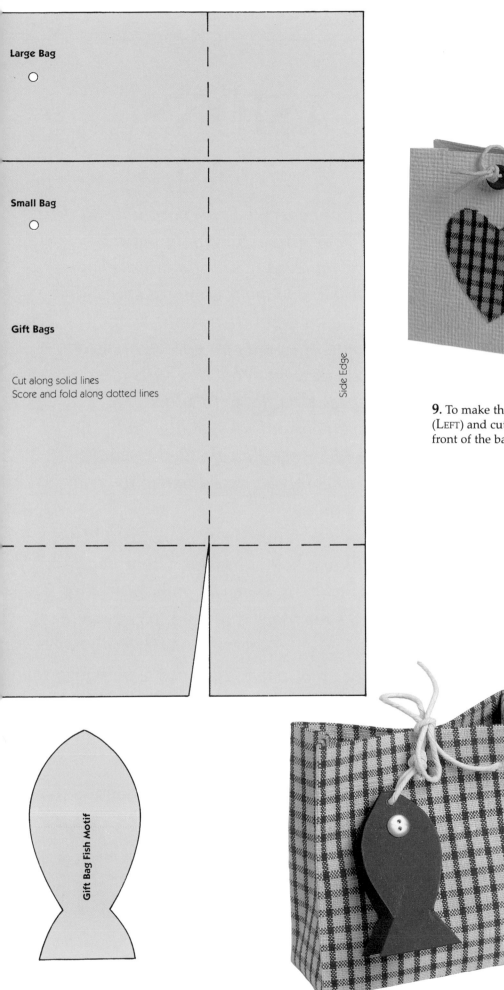

Gift Bag Fish Motif

9. To make the fish and heart decorations, trace the motifs (LEFT) and cut out the shapes in fabric or card. Fix them to the front of the bag with adhesive or double-sided tape.

SPECIAL OCCASIONS

One of the secrets of success is to coordinate all the elements of your gifts – wrapping paper, ribbon, tag, and card. Even if you use shop-bought paper try to make each gift special by adding your own decoration to the shop-bought elements. Presents for special occasions require a little thought. Wedding gifts are often wrapped in white, with silver decorations. Look out for metallic and voile ribbons and for silk flowers, which can be added to a plainly wrapped parcel to make a pretty bouquet.

It is, however, sometimes more fun to try something a little unusual. Crepe papers are available in some rich, vibrant colors, and you can sometimes find these papers with a contrasting color on the reverse, which are especially useful for simple tags. Cover boxes with brightly colored crepe paper, then cut a strip of a contrasting color, long enough to go around the box. Slightly stretch this strip to give it a wavy, crinkled edge, and then wrap this band around the center of the parcel before decorating with colored paper flowers.

WEDDING INVITATION

This elegant design would be perfect for a wedding invitation, but the card would be just as suitable for Mother's Day or for sending someone Easter greetings. The pattern is made from a rubber stamp, but the finished card requires the use of several techniques to give this lovely effect of stained glass. You will need to heat the embossing powder – a hand-held paint stripper is ideal – but take care that it does not become too hot.

60

YOU WILL NEED

Oval floral frame rubber
  stamp
Embossing ink
Tracing paper, 5 × 3¼in
Gold embossing powder
Heat source
Watercolor paints
Paintbrush

White card, 11 × 4in
Yellow mulberry paper,
  5½ × 3¾in
Clear, all-purpose adhesive
Cream card, 5 × 3¼in
Deckle-edged scissors

2. Place the tracing paper face down on a piece of light colored scrap paper, and use watercolor paints to color in the design from the back.

1. Use the embossing ink to print the floral frame stamp onto the tracing paper. Before the ink is dry, sprinkle over the gold embossing powder, tap off the excess and apply heat to emboss the powder.

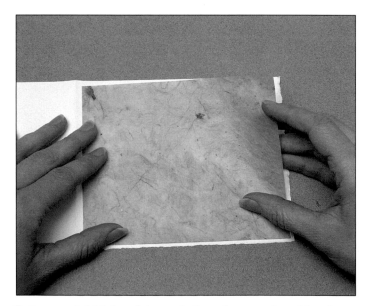

3. Score and fold the white card. Open it out and position the yellow mulberry paper on the front half. Glue in place.

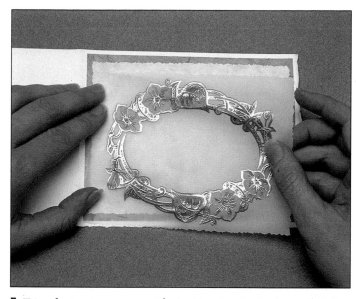

4. Trim the cream card with the deckle-edged scissors. Do not cut too much off – there should be an even border of yellow showing all around when you glue the cream card into place on the mulberry paper.

5. Trim the tracing paper with deckle-edged scissors so that it is the same size as the cream card. Carefully glue it to the card.

61

FABRIC-TRIMMED CARDS

Fabric braids and trimmings make it possible to create some unusually textured cards. You do not have to buy special lengths, although it is worth looking out for unusual braids for particular occasions. Rich reds and golds have been used here, which makes the cards suitable for a wedding anniversary, especially when they are used on deep red card.

YOU WILL NEED

Different types of braids
PVA adhesive or double-sided adhesive tape
Old paintbrush
Fabric cutting scissors
Dark red card, 6 × 4in

62

1. Choose the different braids and cut them to size.

2. Arrange the braids on the cards and stick them down. You can apply adhesive directly to the back of the braid or, if you prefer, use double-sided adhesive tape.

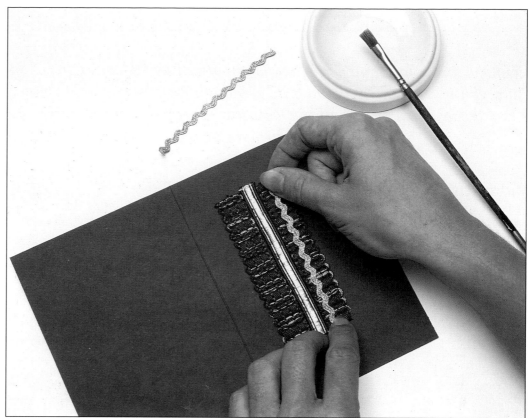

3. Build up layers of different colors and textures. If you have used adhesive, leave it to dry for about 1 hour.

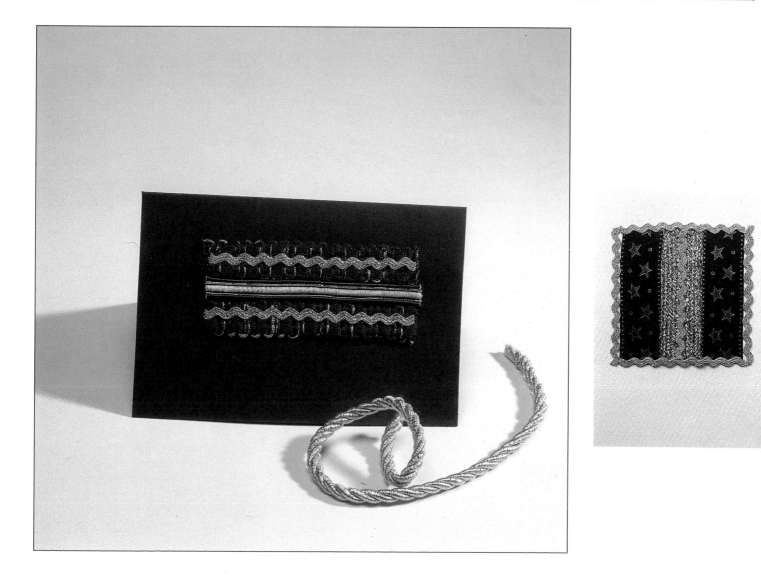

PRESENTATION ENVELOPE

How a card is presented is often as important as the card itself. Simply handing the card over in a plain envelope can seem a little thoughtless, especially if the occasion is an important one. So here is an attractive and versatile way to make a presentation envelope. Note how the lock is symmetrical, no matter which edge is folded first.

YOU WILL NEED

Sheet of stiff paper
Pencil
Ruler
Pair of compasses

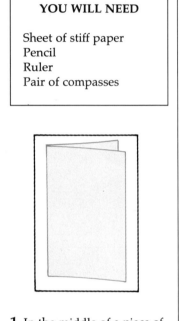

1. In the middle of a piece of stiff paper, draw a line around the card, a little distance away from it, to compensate for the card's thickness.

2. Remove the card and extend the horizontal and vertical lines on the inside of the card. Draw the diagonals to locate the center.

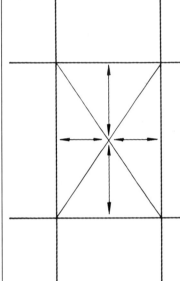

3. Measure the distances from the center point to the edges of the card outline.

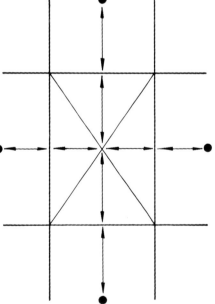

4. Reproduce these distances beyond the central rectangle. Mark the four points with dots. The location of the four outer dots is critical. From this point on, the shapes of the locking flaps can be altered – this is just one way.

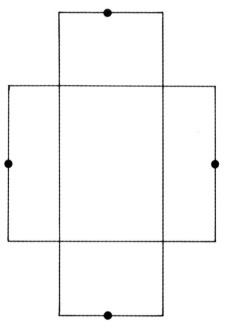

5. Draw rectangles passing through the outer dots. Keep the edges parallel and the corners square.

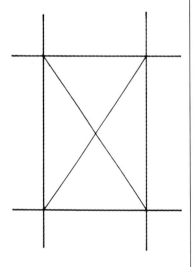

6. Use a pair of compasses to draw the shapes of four quarter circles so that they protrude from the four rectangular flaps. Note that the center of each quarter circle is one of the dots located in step 4 and that they lie to the right of the dot, working clockwise. Cut out the complete shape.

7. Fold in one edge.

9. Fold in the third edge, tucking it under the quarter circle opposite the first edge.

8. Fold in the next edge, working anticlockwise.

10. Fold in the fourth edge, folding it over the third and under the first.

STAMPED HEARTS

It is possible to make stamping tools from a variety of materials, including card, potato, and sponge. For this card corks were used, which, unlike potatoes, do not deteriorate over time, so you can use and reuse them whenever you want. This particular design is for a wedding card. The stamped patterns form a circle that is symbolic of fidelity and perpetual renewal. You could incorporate names or dates into the design or even paste a small photograph into the center of the circle.

YOU WILL NEED

2 corks from wine bottles
Fine marker pen
Craft knife or scalpel
Pair of compasses
White crayon
Blue sugar paper, about
  6 × 4in

Palette or saucer
Gouache paint: white
Silver ink
Silver pen
White card, about
  11½ × 8¼in

66

1. Draw your chosen motif on the corks and use a scalpel or craft knife to remove the areas surrounding the motifs. Do this carefully so that the edge of the pattern stands proud of the top of the corks.

2. Use compasses or a small jar to draw a circle on the paper you intend to print on. The circle is a guide for positioning the printed shapes, so do not press on heavily.

3. Place some white paint and some silver ink on a palette or on a saucer. Dip one of the cork stamps into the paint and the other in the ink, and carefully apply the stamps around the circle, alternating the patterns. When you have completed the circle of stamps, leave the paint to dry for about 10 minutes.

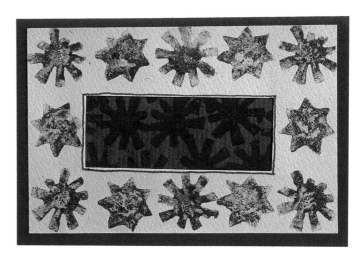

4. Add any further details to the pattern with a silver pen before sticking the pattern to the front of a folded, contrasting piece of card.

WEDDING BELLS

This design is made from more than one piece of card, which allows greater freedom in the design – and it means that it does not have to be as precisely cut as some pop-up designs. The grid is drawn to a scale of 1:2.

YOU WILL NEED

Backing sheet (thick green reflecting foil card), 12¾ × 7½in
Adhesive tape
Thick green reflective card (for supports), about 6 × 6in

Thin silver card (for bell), about 7 × 6in
Scissors
Craft knife or scalpel
Clear, all-purpose adhesive

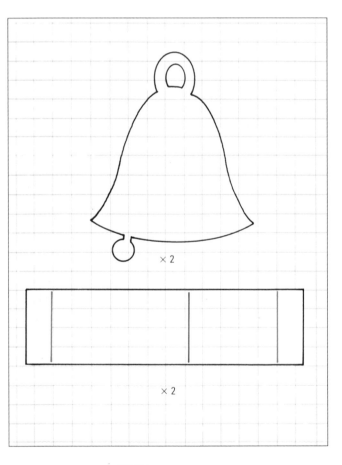

× 2

× 2

KEY

—— cut along this line

—— mountain crease

—— valley crease

▭ glue here (sometimes on the underside)

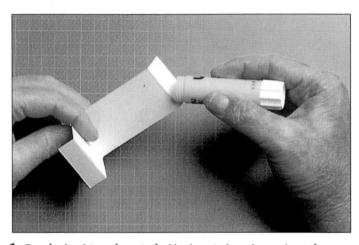

1. Cut the backing sheet in half, place it face down, butt the cut edges together, and stick them together with tape so that it will lie flat after being folded. Use the template (LEFT) to cut out the pieces. Apply glue to the tabs at each end of the support.

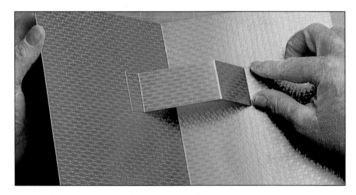

2. Fix the support to the backing sheet.

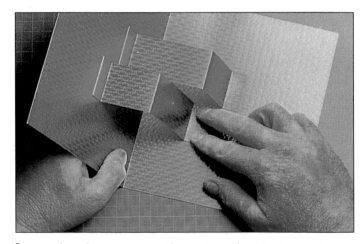

3. Glue the other support to the backing sheet, but reversing the tabs.

4. Glue a bell to one of the supports.

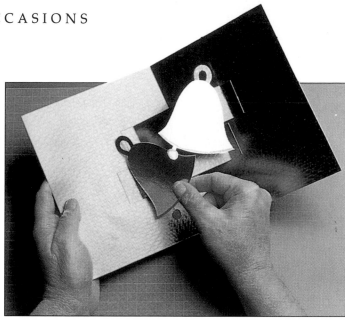

5. Glue the other bell to the other support.

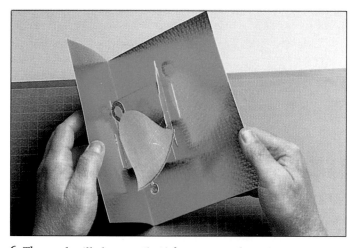

6. The card will close easily if the supports have been accurately positioned.

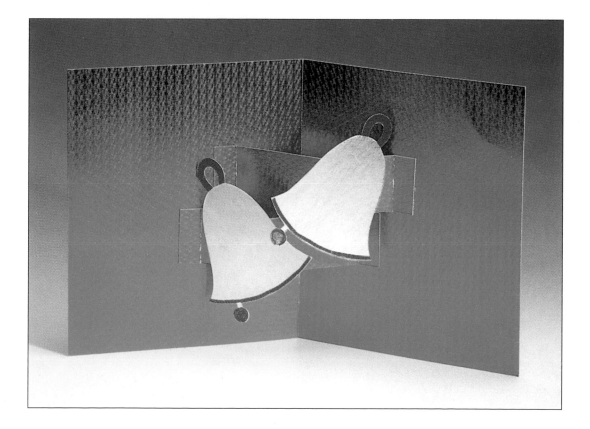

HINGED SHELL GIFT BOX

Natural shells can be hinged together to make enchanting gift boxes, particularly for small items of jewelry.

YOU WILL NEED

Large scallop shell or
    lucina shell
Sheet of medium-grade
    sandpaper

PVA glue
Small brass hinge

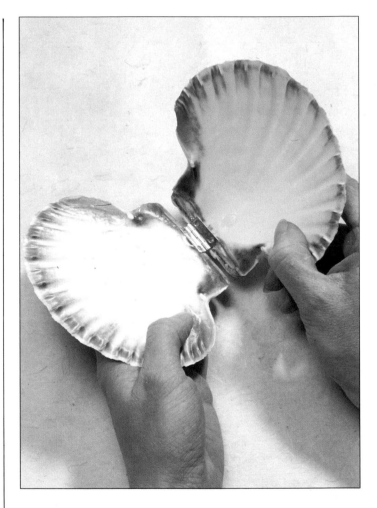

1. Wash and dry the shell carefully. Place the two halves together to give you an indication to where the hinge should be positioned. Rub the surface of the shell at the hinge position with sandpaper. This will smooth the area and provide a good surface for the glue to adhere to.

2. Glue one side of the hinge into position and allow the glue to set firmly. Glue the other side in place. Allow the glue to set completely before flexing the hinge.

WEDDING GIFTS

A home made cracker makes a very special gift. The method is shown on page 118. Choose the materials and colors to reflect the occasion – in this case pastel and white papers. The traditional wedding almonds are tied in white net and placed on decorated crepe paper.

ROSE PETAL CONFETTI

What could be more romantic – and ecologically sound – than to use real rose petals for confetti? Their random sizes, lovely soft colors, and delicate perfume take them into a different league from the more usual paper variety, and they will be the perfect finishing touch for a special day. The rose petals were dried in silica gel, so that they did not lose their color, shape, and perfume. Pack the confetti into pretty handmade boxes, tied with ribbon, raffia, or colored string. These little boxes would also be perfect for holding little gifts – candies or homemade pot pourri, for example. Just change the color scheme to suit the occasion.

YOU WILL NEED

About two full-blown roses for each box
Silica gel crystals
Small ovenproof dish
Spoon
Large sheet of petal paper (available commercially)
Sharp scissors
Double-sided adhesive tape
Paper punch
Small piece of thin card
Tracing paper
About 12in narrow ribbon

2. Place the dish in the oven at its lowest possible setting and leave for about 20 minutes. Check at intervals. When the petals are dry the crystals will have turned white. Remove the dish from the oven and leave to cool. Take the petals from the dish – be careful because they will be fragile – gently tapping excess powder from the petals. You may find that a soft paintbrush is helpful for brushing away any crystals that cling.

1. Carefully remove the petals from the rose. Sprinkle a layer of silica gel crystals into the base of an ovenproof dish. Add a layer of rose petals and spoon over more crystals. Continue to add layers of petals and crystals until the dish is full and the petals are completely covered.

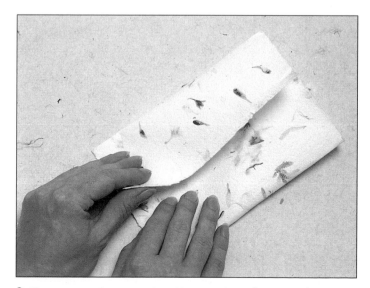

3. Cut a rectangle measuring 12 × 8in from the large sheet of paper. Fold the short edges of the rectangle towards the center, and overlap by ½in. Hold the overlap in place with double-sided adhesive tape.

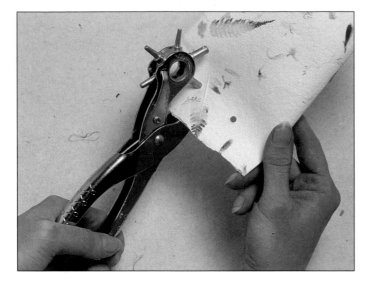

4. Use the paper punch to make two holes at the top opening for the ribbon bow.

5. Using the outline (BELOW LEFT), copy and transfer the outline of the base of the box to the thin card and cut out the shape. Score and fold the dotted lines. Use double-sided tape to hold the base in position. Fill the box with the rose petals, then thread the ribbon through the punched holes and tie with a bow.

Enlarge by 25% on a photocopier to trace at full size

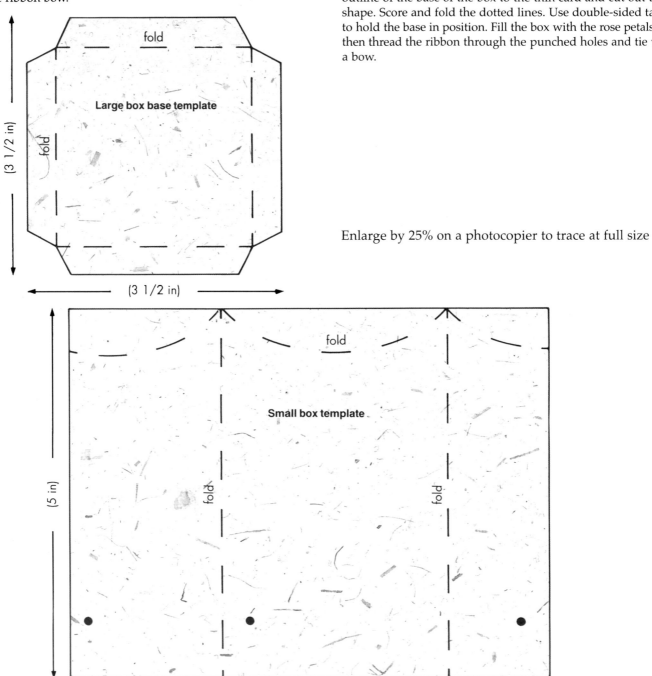

fold

Large box base template

(3 1/2 in)

fold

(3 1/2 in)

fold

Small box template

(5 in)

fold

fold

(6 1/2 in)

SMALL BOX

Cut out the shape of the box from petal paper, using the template on page 74. Score along the dotted lines. Fold the sides inward so that they overlap at the center, and hold them in place with double-sided tape. Use a paper punch to make a hole at the center of the top edge. Fold the curved semicircular sections to form the bottom, and hold them together with a small piece of double-sided tape. Fill with rose petals, and tie with a ribbon bow.

PERFECT PAPER

Paper is a very versatile medium. You can create wonderful three-dimensional and textured effects with simple techniques. Both children and adults will enjoy cutting and folding, creasing and curling, and pleating papers to create original and inexpensive gift wrappings for special occasions. You will need some fine to medium weight papers in a range of colors, scissors or a scalpel, a cutting mat, and clear, all-purpose adhesive or double-sided tape.

A simple cut-out pattern of little regularly spaced squares, cut on three sides, gives an interesting effect for little effort. Lightly draw a grid on the reverse of the paper, and carefully cut the squares, making sure that the cut lines do not run into each other.

A more complicated effect can be achieved by marking a diagonal grid on the reverse of the paper. If you cut the diagonals of the squares, rather than the outlines of the squares, you can achieve a rather mysterious effect.

LEFT: Lightly fold plain paper around the box. Lay it flat again, and mark out the circular pattern on two of the box sides only. Cut out the pattern with a scalpel. Wrap the box and decorate with shredded paper and a gift tag decorated in the same way.

A small gift can look effective by cutting a pattern in only part of the paper. Add a similarly decorated tag and matching corkscrews of paper. A colored box showing through the cut paper creates an interesting effect.

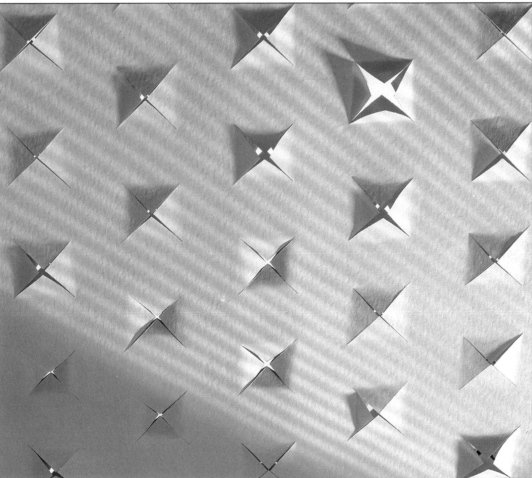

Continue the white paper theme with a card made by folding some handmade or embossed paper in half. Cut a "vase" from plain white paper, and cut some rows of small Vs across the top. Glue the side of the vase to the card, then cut some flower and leaf shapes from white paper and glue them to the card so that they seem to be growing inside the vase.

A pretty wrapping for a wedding present could be made from medium weight white paper. Make a repeating pattern of triangles, but cut only the sloping sides, not the base. Finish off with a decorative bow made by folding strips of white paper and gluing them to the top of the present. When you are cutting out these paper patterns you must use a sharp blade so that every line is clean and sharp. Use the point of a scalpel to lift the points of the triangles away from the backing.

CHRISTMAS AND
— NEW YEAR —

In spite of the ever-increasing range of colorful and well-designed cards and wrapping papers that are available, there is still nothing to equal the homemade version. A Christmas card is always appreciated even more when it has been made by hand, and imaginative gift wraps make any gift, no matter how small, more special. In the following section are dozens of ideas for adding a personal style to cards and parcels. They range from quick, simple ideas to more complicated projects for the special people on your Christmas list. Children can make and help with many of the ideas, and will enjoy the sponging, spattering, or potato printing.

There is, in addition, an enormous range of ribbons and papers available, and you will also find plenty of ideas for using them in unusual and intriguing ways. Remember, too, that a gift can be wrapped in fabric to make a change from paper-wrapped presents. Tartan fabrics have wonderfully rich colors and textures, and you can complement the natural look by adding bows of cotton braids and ribbon in dark, warm colors. Fresh berries, nuts, and pine cones are wonderful accompaniments. Keep a look out for remnants of fabrics in haberdashery shops, because these are often large enough for a parcel but much less expensive than specially bought lengths. Keep all your odd scraps of fabric, because you can always use them to make small bags for dried lavender or soap or to tie into bows.

POTATO PRINTS

One of the advantages of potato prints is that it is possible to make several cards from one potato. The technique could hardly be simpler or less expensive, and it is suitable for children, although they may need help cutting the shape in the potato. Choose simple, bold motifs — potato prints are not going to give you wonderfully subtle images! Use textured paper or create an interesting base paper by spattering paint finely over the paper before you apply the potato motifs. Any thickness of paper can be used, but tissue paper works surprisingly well.

YOU WILL NEED

Colored card, 8 × 4in
Thin card for templates
Scissors
Pencil or fine pen

Large potato
Sharp kitchen knife
Gouache or poster paints
Saucer or palette

1. Fold the card in half. Draw on a piece of spare card the outline of a star, Christmas tree, bell, or holly leaf, and cut around the outline to make a template.

2. Cut a large potato in half and press it against a paper towel to remove some of the moisture.

3. Use a pencil or fine marker pen to draw around your card template to transfer the image to the surface of the potato.

4. With a small kitchen knife, carefully cut around the shape. Take care that you do not mark or damage the surface of the image.

5. Dilute some gouache or poster paint in a saucer or palette and dip the surface of the potato into the paint. Press the potato firmly down on a piece of scrap paper.

6. If the shape is not fully printed, dry the paint off and carefully slice off part of the image to give a flatter surface.

7. Use the potato to print as many cards as you like. We added a border of printed strips by cutting a long, thin piece of potato so that the border had the same kind of surface texture as the printed image.

COLLAGE STAR

A creative painting technique is used to produce richly colored backgrounds on which to build layers of different papers. The end result is an unusual and individual greeting card. Collect foil paper, Christmas wrapping paper, and metallic papers for this project, and choose your paints to complement the foil. The paints used are rich purple and turquoise, and the gold star helps to create an unusual but attractive Christmas card.

YOU WILL NEED

Household sponge
Gouache paint: turquoise,
   ultramarine, purple
Palette or saucer
Garden water spray
Watercolor paper
   11½ × 8¼in
Gold ink
Paintbrush

Foil papers: various colors
Scissors
Clear, all-purpose adhesive
Gold card
Ruler and pencil
White card, about
   12 × 8in
Gold pen

2. Select your paint colors and place them on a palette or saucer. Mist the piece of watercolor paper with water, then apply the paint to the paper using pieces of sponge.

1. Tear a household sponge into small pieces so that you can use a separate piece for each color.

3. Mist the painted surface with water again, and use a clean piece of sponge to blend the colors together.

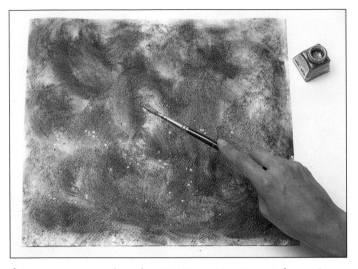

4. Load a paintbrush with gold ink and tap it over the surface of the paint to give a stippled effect. Leave to dry for 20–30 minutes.

84

5. Select different colors of foil papers, cut them to the size you want and crumple them in your hands.

6. Glue the layers together. The largest piece, part of the painted paper, which has been torn to size, goes at the bottom, with the foil papers next, and a smaller piece, torn from the painted paper, on top.

7. Draw a small star on a piece of gold card, cut it out and stick it to the center of the collage.

8. Glue the finished collage to a larger piece of contrasting card. Fold the card so that the collage is on the front, then draw a gold border with a fine pen to finish the design.

STENCILED CHRISTMAS TREE

This is a quick and easy card to make, but the technique can be adapted to make more complicated images. You can, for example, spray the stencil several times to give an overlaid effect, or you could cut several stencils and combine them to create patterns and pictures. Remember to work in a well-ventilated room when you use spray paints – better still, work outdoors if possible.

YOU WILL NEED

Stiff card for stencil,
  4¾ × 3½in
Tracing paper
Ruler and pencil
Craft knife

Red cartridge paper
Gold spray paint
Fine gold marker pen
Clear, all-purpose adhesive
Dark green card, 6 × 4in

86

1. Draw the Christmas tree motif on the stiff card, making sure that there is at least ¾in all around the design.

2. Use a craft knife to cut out the motifs. Rest your work on a special cutting mat or thick card to protect your work surface.

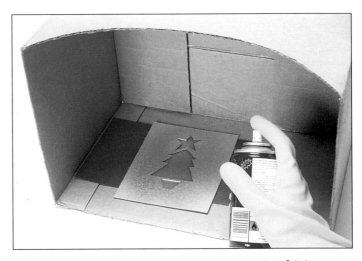

3. To protect the surroundings, make a "spray booth" from a cardboard box. Place the stencil over the cartridge paper and spray over the stencil with gold paint.

4. Allow the paint to dry (about 5 minutes) before tearing the paper to size.

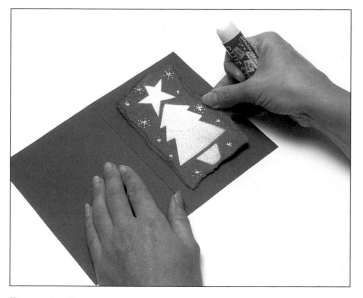

5. Add further decorative elements with a gold pen. Take the piece of paper and glue it to the front of the card.

6. Finish off by drawing in a gold border.

STENCILED WREATH

The two-part stencil used on this card was a ready-made wreath of holly leaves, which is perfect for a delicate Christmas card. Most craft shops stock a range of stencils, many made of waxed card or even thin metal, but before you buy, make sure that the pattern will be suitable for the card you want to make. On well-made two-part stencils, the first image is cut out and the complete second image is drawn in with dotted lines. The dotted lines are invaluable when you come to line up the second image.

YOU WILL NEED

Plain blank cards, white
Ready-made wreath
   stencil
Saucers or palettes

Stencil or acrylic paint:
   red, green
Stencil brushes

88

1. Separate the two parts of the stencil and put small amounts of red and green paint in different saucers.

2. Place the first stencil in position over the card and dip your brush in the green paint. Blot it on a paper towel to make sure that it is not too wet, then move it confidently around the cut-out several times, working in the same direction.

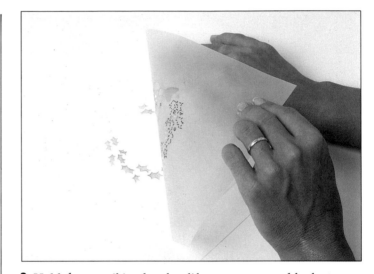

3. Hold the stencil in place but lift up a corner and look at your efforts. If the image is not strong enough, replace the stencil and continue to build up the color.

4. When you are satisfied with the green, remove the stencil and leave the paint to dry completely before placing the second stencil over the first image. The bow and berries of the wreath are cut out of this stencil, but the leaves are shown as dotted lines so that you can align it accurately. Stencil the second image.

5. If you are making several cards, it is a sensible idea to stencil all the green sections first.

6. When the green paint is dry, add the red part of the pattern to all the cards. You could also add a detail of the design to the envelopes.

STAMPED CHRISTMAS TREE

Printing stamps can be used either with an ink pad or by using water-based, felt-tipped pens, which are applied directly to the stamp. We have decorated this simple Christmas tree in both ways to show how easy it is. Although we used a fairly large stamp – the image is about 5in high – a smaller version of this would be ideal for making gift tags.

YOU WILL NEED

Rubber stamp
Ink pad or range of
 water-based felt-
 tipped pens
Cream card, about 8 ×
 6in
Felt-tipped pens,
 watercolor paints, or
 crayons
Glitter glue or clear
 adhesive and loose
 glitter

2. Print the stamp by placing it straight down on the card. Apply the necessary pressure – a delicate pattern will require little pressure, but a bolder design will need to be pressed down quite firmly. Avoid rocking the stamp from side to side, because this will blur the finished image.

USING AN INK PAD

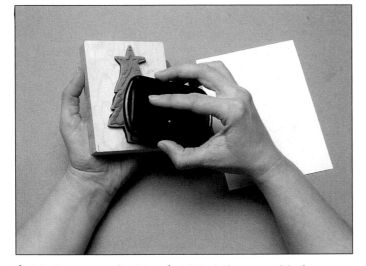

1. Ink the stamp, checking that it is fully covered before printing. When you are using a larger stamp such as this tree, it is often easier to apply the pad to the stamp, rather than vice versa, because this helps to avoid the ink overflowing, especially if you are using pigment inks.

3. Remove the stamp by lifting it straight up.

1. Once the stamp has been printed, additional color can be added to finish the decoration. You can use felt-tipped pens, watercolor paints, or even ordinary colored crayons.

USING FELT-TIPPED PENS

1. Use a felt-tipped pen to apply color directly to the stamp. An advantage of using felt-tipped pens is that you can use several colors at any one time. You must work quickly, however, so that the ink does not dry.

2. Glitter glue can be applied straight from the tube to add sparkling effects to the tree – we used red for the baubles and gold to add highlights to the star.

2. Before printing the stamp, moisten any dried ink by "huffing" on the image. Print in the normal way.

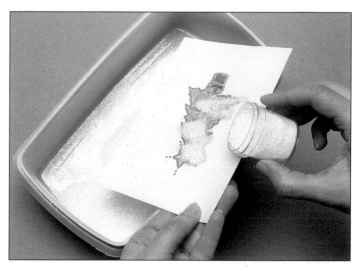

3. Alternatively, apply a few spots of adhesive and, before the glue begins to set, scatter loose glitter over the card, shaking off the excess into a tray or onto a large sheet of paper so that you can return it to the container.

91

POINSETTIA WREATH CARD

This pretty card is made by using a simple rubber stamp and by the additional techniques of embossing and hand coloring with felt-tipped pens.

YOU WILL NEED

Embossing pad
Poinsettia wreath rubber
  stamp
Cream card, 5½ × 4in
Black embossing powder
Heat source
Felt-tipped pens: red,

bright green, dark green
Embossing ink
Fine paintbrush
Turquoise card, about
  10¼ ×6¼in
Clear embossing powder

1. Ink the stamp with the embossing ink and print the image onto the piece of cream card.

3. Use a hand-held paint stripper to heat the embossing powder. Take care that it does not become too hot.

2. Before the ink dries, pour over the black embossing powder. Tap off any excess powder into a bowl.

4. Color in the embossed design with felt-tipped pens.

5. Use a fine paintbrush to paint a thin coat of embossing ink over the colored areas.

6. Sprinkle clear embossing powder over the surface of the inked area, tap off any excess, and heat carefully. Finish the card by positioning the cream card in the center of the scored and folded turquoise card.

CANNED CHRISTMAS CARDS

These unusual cards are made from pieces of old tin cans. They are fun and easy to make, but take care when you are cutting and working with metal, and always wear protective gloves because the edges can be sharp. When you are punching out the designs, use a thick piece of card to protect your work surface. The metal we used came from the side of a large, empty coffee can. Use tin-snips to remove the bottom and top of the can, then cut down the side and open it out to form a flat sheet.

94

YOU WILL NEED

Tracing paper
Pencil
Ruler
Scalpel or craft knife
Colored card, some with
    textured surface
Pieces of tin
Masking tape
Small hammer
Center punch
Tin snips
Double-sided adhesive
    tape

1. Trace the templates for the cards and motifs (pages 96, 97), making sure that you transfer all cutting lines and fold lines, too. The dots on the motif outlines indicate the positions of the punched holes. Cut the basic card shape, then cut out the windows, using a craft knife or scalpel and a metal ruler. Score and fold the card along the fold lines.

2. Choose a motif, then cut a piece of metal about 1in larger all round than the motif. Place the piece of metal on thick card and place the traced motif on top, holding the tracing in place with masking tape. Place the point of the center punch on each dot and tap once or twice with a hammer. The aim is to make a neat dent in the surface of the metal but not to pierce a hole right through. Continue until the motif is complete, then remove the tracing.

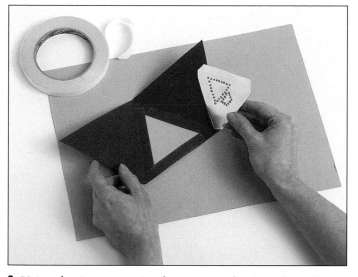

3. Using the tin-snips, trim the metal so that it is about ½in larger all round than the window cut in the card. Attach the metal, face down behind the window, using double-sided tape to hold it in place.

4. Fold over the left-hand side of the card to cover the back of the metal piece. Hold it in place with double-sided tape.

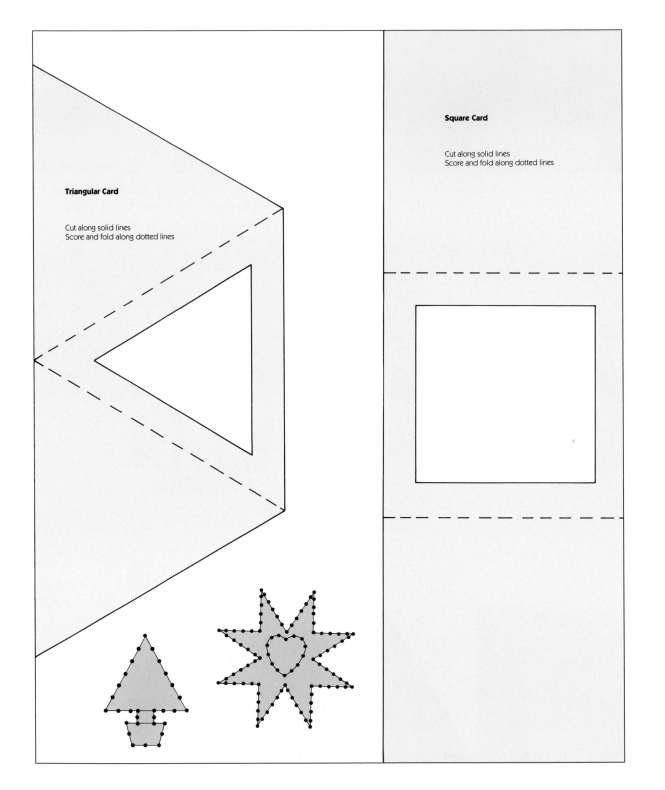

Triangular Card

Cut along solid lines
Score and fold along dotted lines

Square Card

Cut along solid lines
Score and fold along dotted lines

Enlarge all templates by 33% on a photocopier to trace at full size

Rectangular Card

Cut along solid lines
Score and fold along dotted lines

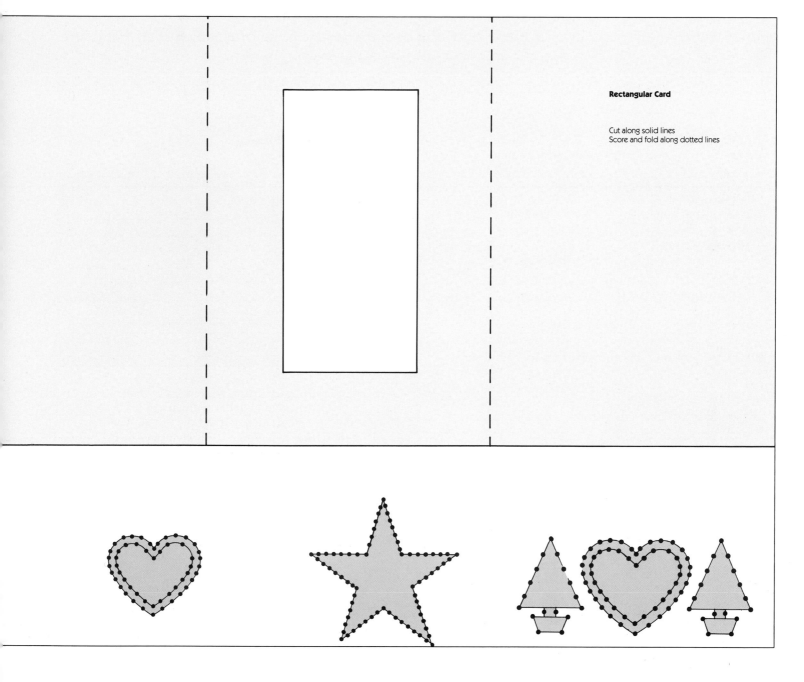

STENCILED INVITATIONS AND PLACE CARDS

Gold on ivory-colored card is a sophisticated combination for these elegant invitation cards and place cards. The patterns are stenciled onto the plain card, but you could also stencil the motifs onto plain paper napkins and even a white tablecloth for a wholly coordinated look. Use a paint that is specially designed for stenciling, because it is quick drying, but remember to wash the brushes, sponges and mixing palette as soon as you have finished, so that the paint does not harden and become almost impossible to remove.

YOU WILL NEED

Tracing paper	heavy watercolor paper
Pencil	Gold stencil paint
Thick card	Saucer or palette
Clear acetate stencil film	Sponge
Masking tape	Ruler
Scalpel or craft knife	Blunt table knife
Leather punch	Metallic gold pen
Textured paper, such as	

Enlarge by 50% on a photocopier to trace at full size

1. Trace the templates (LEFT) and place the traced motif on a piece of thick card. Place a piece of acetate film over the tracing and hold the two together with tabs of masking tape. Use a scalpel or craft knife to cut out the design. The star and heart are the easiest to cut out. The holly leaves involve more curved lines, and the most difficult is the little gift. To begin with, cut only the ribbon of the gift.

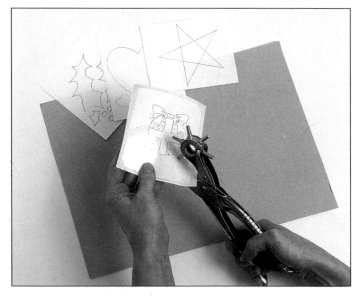

2. Use a leather punch to cut the tiny dots in the gift stencil. Little holes like this would be impossible to cut in any other way.

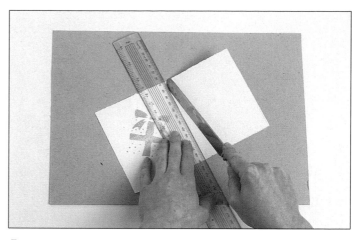

5. Using a ruler and a blunt table knife, score along the halfway point measured in step 3. Then score halfway across the front section, above and below the stenciled motif but not across the design itself.

3. Make each invitation from a piece of paper measuring 8 × 4½in. Mark the halfway point lightly with a pencil line. Place the stencil in the center of the left-hand side of the paper. Put a little paint in a saucer or palette. Take a piece of sponge and press the surface onto the paint, taking care that you do not overload the sponge. Press the sponge lightly on the stencil, using a dabbing action. Let the paint dry before you remove the stencil.

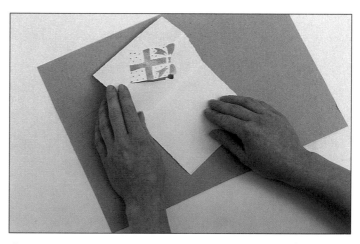

6. Fold the paper along the fold lines so that the motif stands out of the folded front part and creates a very simple three-dimensional effect.

4. Beginning at the top of the stenciled pattern, halfway across the front section of the paper, use the scalpel or craft knife to cut carefully around the right-hand side of the design. Stop when you reach the bottom, again about half-way across the front portion.

7. Make each place card from a square of paper measuring about 4¾ × 4¾in. Mark the halfway point, then stencil the design as before, but position the motif slightly to the left of center. Score across the halfway point, avoiding the stencil. Write a name on the card with a metallic pen, then fold back the top half of the card.

CHRISTMAS STOCKING

Children love finding a stocking of presents on Christmas morning. They are simple to make and you can use any material you have to hand. Decorate them with buttons, beads, and ribbon. Each stocking is approximately 1ft 3¾in long and 10in wide at the base of the foot.

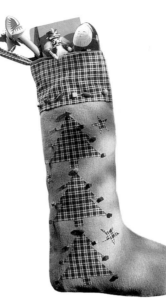

1. Make the basic stocking in yellow fabric with a contrasting blue checked top and Christmas tree.

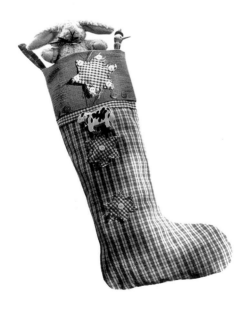

2. Use blue checked fabric as the base and add a green top and details in red checked fabric.

3. Make a blue and tartan stocking. Add a tartan pocket and bows made from checked cloth and raffia.

ADVENT CALENDAR

Children will love this Christmas tree Advent calendar, complete with shining star a host of chirpy robins and a pile of little gifts. Each one hides a box containing candies or a small surprise and has a number to correspond to each of the days up to Christmas.

YOU WILL NEED

Stiff card, green, white, and red
Pencil
Scissors
Double-sided adhesive tape
Double-sided adhesive pads
Dark fiber tip pen
Assorted scraps of paper,

brown, red, black, gold, etc
Scraps of corrugated card (red, green)
Narrow ribbons, assorted colors
Craft knife
Double-sided adhesive Velcro fastening
Adhesive numbers

2. Attach the tree and the pot to the background, using double-sided adhesive pads. This will give a slightly three-dimensional effect.

1. To make the tree and background, trace the template pieces full size, using the grid given on page 105. Each square represents 2in. First cut out the snow from the white card and use double-sided tape to secure it in place on the large blue background board. Then cut out the pot from red card, and the tree from green.

3. To make the robins, trace the robin template shapes given on page 105. You will need to make 12 robins. Cut the main body in brown, the wings in black, and the chest in red. Remember that the robins need to face each other, so make six that look to the left, and six that look to the right.

4. Assemble the robins, using double-sided adhesive tape.

5. When the robins are complete, draw in the eyes with a dark fiber tip pen.

6. To make the boxes, trace the box tray and sleeve templates on page 105. Cut 24 trays in white card, 13 sleeves in green card and 11 sleeves in white. Score and fold where indicated. Make up the box trays and fix with double-sided tape.

7. Using double-sided tape, attach the green sleeves as shown to the back of the robins and the star, and save the white ones to attach to the gifts (step 8).

8. To make the gifts, cut six squares 2¾ × 2¾ inches and five rectangles 2 × 2¾ inches from stiff white card. Cover the squares and rectangles with scraps of corrugated card etc, then tie each with a ribbon bow. Attach a box to the back of each gift as before.

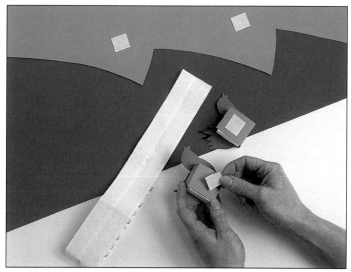

9. Cut 24 pieces of Velcro, each ½ inch long. Separate the hook side from the loop side and fix one to the back of each box sleeve and the other to the calendar. Use the photograph as a guide to positioning.

10. Trace the star template given on page 105. Cut out in gold card and attach a box to the back.

11. Stick a number on each of the robins and the gifts but make the star number 24. Secure each piece in place on the calendar, and then count the days to Christmas.

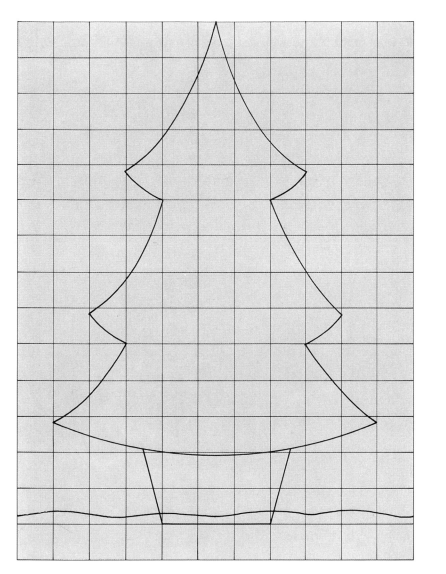

Each square represents 2in

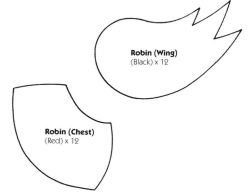

Cut along solid lines

Score along folded lines

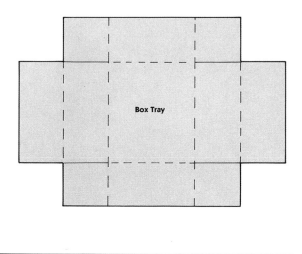

Enlarge templates on a photocopier by 33% to trace at full size

NATURAL CHRISTMAS CARDS AND GIFT TAGS

Let nature help when it comes to decorating cards and gift tags. Collect dried fruit slices, spices, leaves, and seeds and arrange them on different kinds of paper. Some of the most successful designs are made simply by lining up spices or seeds in rows or spirals around an interesting shape – a piece of dried fruit or a leaf, for example – so use your imagination to create a multitude of designs. Use a handmade paper with a deckled edge, use a pair of deckle-edged scissors, or tear the edge carefully so that it has the same effect.

YOU WILL NEED

Assorted papers,
 including handmade or
 textured papers
Sharp scissors
Double-sided adhesive
 tape
Quick-drying adhesive
Selection of cloves, tiny
 chiles, sycamore keys,
 dried fruit slices, star
 anise, cinnamon bark,
 dried bay leaves
Paper punch
Fine string or twine

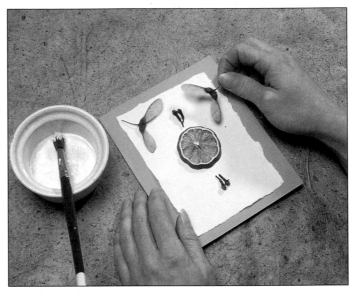

2. Arrange the dried fruit, seeds, and so forth on the front of the card. When you are happy with the arrangement, stick them down with a quick-drying adhesive.

1. Cut a rectangle of paper measuring about 9½ × 6in. Score down the center and fold the paper in half. Take a smaller rectangle of a contrasting paper and fix it to the front with double-sided adhesive tape.

3. Make a matching gift tag in the same way but with a smaller piece of paper – say, a quarter or a third of the size of the main card. Punch a hole in one corner and thread through a length of string or twine so that you can attach the tag to a package.

OH, TANNENBAUM

This pop-up tree is a fairly easy card to make, and you can involve your children in coloring the tree and tub when you have cut them out. This tree was decorated with felt-tipped pens, but you could stick on little pieces of paper and self-adhesive stars and spangles. The grid is drawn to a scale of 1:2.

YOU WILL NEED

Backing sheet (thin gray card glued to mounting card), 8½ × 8in	Thin gray card (for tree and tub), about 10 × 6in
Scissors	Craft knife or scalpel
Adhesive tape	Felt-tipped pens
	Clear, all-purpose adhesive

108

KEY

——————	cut along this line
——————	suggested artwork
——————	mountain crease
——————	valley crease
▭	glue here (sometimes on the underside)

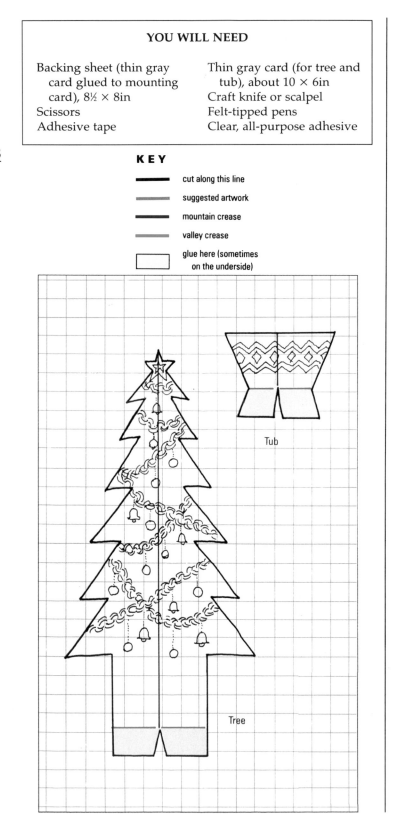

Tub

Tree

1. Cut the backing sheet in half, place it face down, butt the cut edges together, and stick them together with tape so that it will lie flat after being folded. Use the template (LEFT) to cut out the tree and tub. Decorate them, then apply glue to the tree tabs.

2. Glue the tree to the backing sheet, making sure that the center of the tree aligns exactly with the center of the card base.

3. Apply glue to the underside of the tub tabs.

5. When the card is shut, the tree and tub will tip forward.

4. Glue the tub to the backing sheet, making sure to position it a little way in front of the tree.

FESTIVE FIR

Although this pop-up design looks simple, the construction must be very precise so that it will work well. In particular, pay attention to the way the base of the tree pieces glue to the inside of the tub, because the measurements and creasing must be absolutely accurate. You will know when you have got it right because the tree will open gracefully.
The grid is drawn to a scale of 1:2½.

YOU WILL NEED

Backing sheet (thin orange card glued to mounting card), 14½ × 12¾in
Scissors
Adhesive tape
Thick green paper (for tree), about 9 × 8in
Thick brown paper (for tub), about 8 × 5in
Craft knife or scalpel
Clear, all-purpose adhesive

KEY

—— cut along this line

—— mountain crease

—— valley crease

☐ glue here (sometimes on the underside)

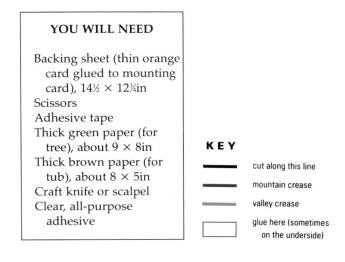

Tree

Tub

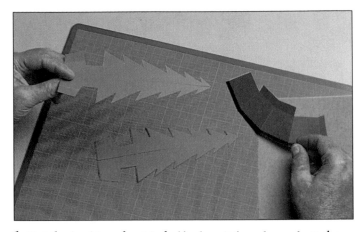

1. Cut the backing sheet in half, place it face down, butt the cut edges together, and stick them with tape so that it will lie flat after being folded. Use the template (LEFT) to cut out the tree pieces and tub. Note the different positions of the slits on the two tree halves.

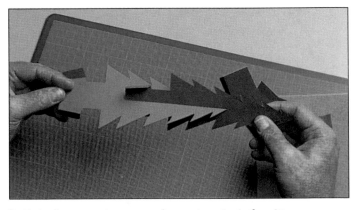

2. Slide the tree pieces together to interlock the slits.

3. Apply glue to the end tab on the tub, then form it into a square tube.

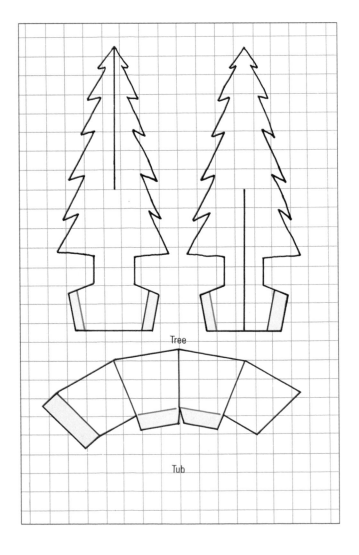

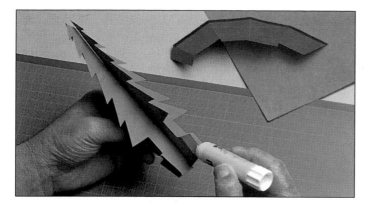

4. Apply glue to the four tabs at the base of the tree.

6. Apply glue to the underside of the tub tabs, then stick the tabs to the backing sheet.

5. Glue the tree inside the tub so that the crease on each tree tab lies exactly down the center of each tub face.

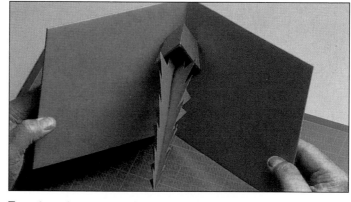

7. Although it is very three-dimensional, the tub and tree will easily collapse flat when the card is closed.

WHERE'S RUDOLPH?

The crease pattern used here to make Santa Claus open out will be familiar to anyone who has ever made an origami water-bomb. Indeed, many origami bases and techniques can be adapted for use in pop-up designs. A close study of the similarities between the two papercrafts can be the source of many inspirational ideas. For best results, place the three creases that run across the figure of Santa Claus very precisely. It would be worth making a rough, undecorated figure to judge the placement of the creases before folding the actual figure.
The grid is drawn to a scale of 1:2.

YOU WILL NEED

Backing sheet (thin blue
  card glued to mounting
  card), 15½ × 7½in
Scissors
Adhesive tape
Craft knife or scalpel

Medium weight white
  paper (for Santa Claus),
  about 11 × 6in
Felt-tipped pens or marker
  pens
Clear, all-purpose adhesive

KEY

—— cut along this line

‑ ‑ ‑ suggested artwork

—— mountain crease

‑ ‑ ‑ valley crease

☐ glue here (sometimes
  on the underside)

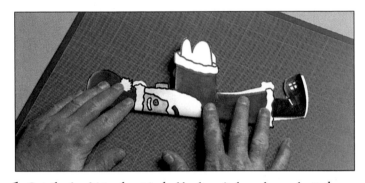

1. Cut the backing sheet in half, place it face down, butt the cut edges together, and stick them together with tape so that it will lie flat after being folded. Use the template (LEFT) to cut out the figure of Santa Claus. Crease the figure down the center. Open it out.

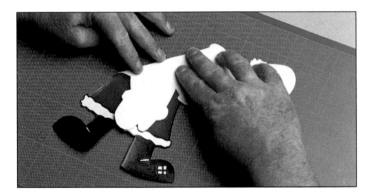

2. With the decorated side upward, crease one of the diagonals. Open out.

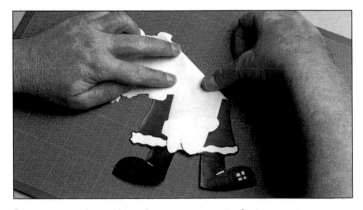

3. Repeat, folding the other diagonal. Both diagonals must cross the center crease at the same point.

112

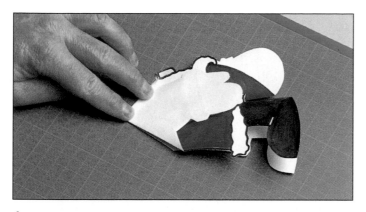

4. Santa will collapse along the creases.

6. Glue the hands to the backing sheet.

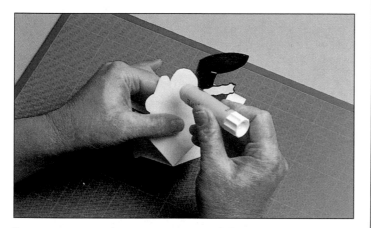

5. Apply glue to the underside of both hands.

7. Note that the card will not open absolutely flat.

TWO-PIECE BOXES

A two-piece box can be a simple tray or it can be a complicated star-shaped box – ideal for a little Christmas gift. Use a fairly stiff card, and either cover it when it is finished or decorate the card before cutting it out.

BASIC BOX

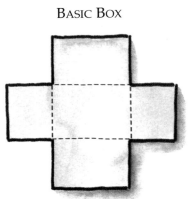

1. The most basic box that you can possibly make is to cut out a cruciform shape to the required size and to stick the sides together with adhesive tape.

2. Make the lid in the same way, but make the sides very short and add about ⅛in (depending on the thickness of the card you are using) to the dimensions in all directions so that the lid will slip over the sides of the box.

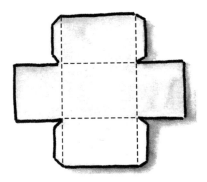

3. A slightly more sophisticated box is made with glued tabs. Make sure that you make the allowance for the lid slightly more than for the simple tray box to accommodate the extra thickness of the flaps.

WRAP-ROUND BOX

1. Make a wrap-round box by marking a strip of card that is equal in length to twice the length and twice the width of the gift, plus a glue flap. The strip can have joins if necessary. Cut out the card, score the folds, and glue to form a box.

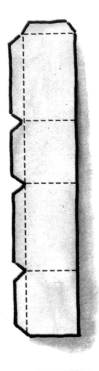

2. The wrap-round lid is made from a piece of card measuring the length of the gift by twice the width and twice the height plus an overlap. Cut out and score the folds.

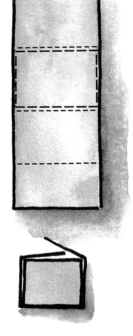

3. Glue the center section of the lid to the glue flap at the base of the box. Fold the side and top pieces around the box, enclosing the gift. Either tie it to close or seal with a sticker.

STAR-SHAPED BOX

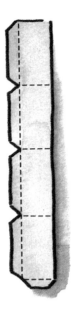

1. Mark out a strip of card, but with the sides of equal length, to form a square. Make the lid in the same way, but slightly larger.

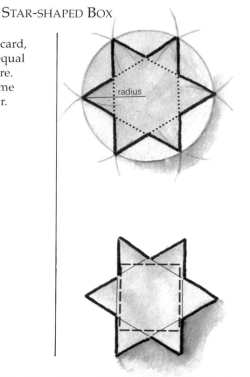

2. To construct the star, measure the length of one side of the box with the compasses to find the radius of the circle. Draw the circle, and, keeping the same radius setting, place the point of the compasses on the circumference of the circle, and mark the point it crosses on the curve. Move the compass to this point, and repeat the process until you have six points around the circumference. Join alternate points with a pencil and ruler.

3. Cut out two star shapes and glue one to the flaps of the base, and the other to the flaps of the top of the lid.

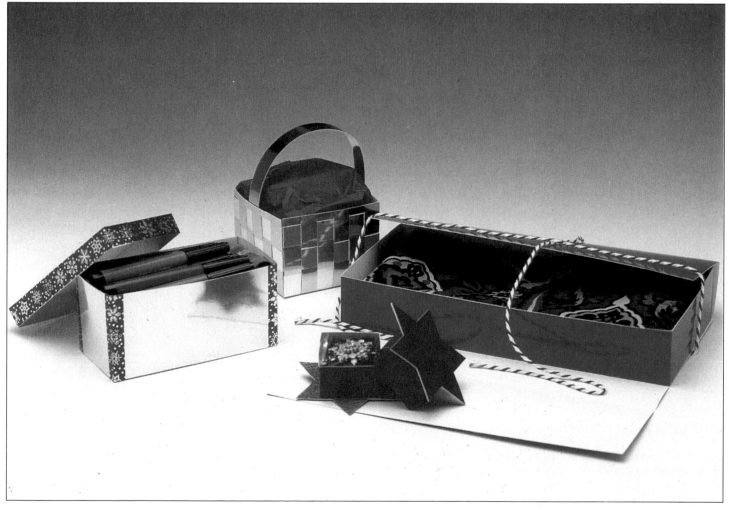

The possibilities for decorating homemade boxes are endless. Decorative adhesive tape, stickers, and attractive ties all contribute to a professional looking gift. The basket-type box was made by weaving strips of metallic-finish card together, with a simple strip attached to act as a handle.

SIMPLE GIFT WRAPS

This is a simple technique for decorating paper, and is suitable for children to try. You can transform sheets of plain, matt construction paper into richly patterned, unusual wrapping paper with very few materials. Gold and red or green always look festive, but you could use silver or red or purple. Remember to finish off the present with matching ribbon.

YOU WILL NEED

Large sheets of plain
   construction paper
Gold poster or acrylic craft
   paint

Saucer or palette
Cloth or tissue paper
Low-tack masking tape
Metallic gold spray paint

116

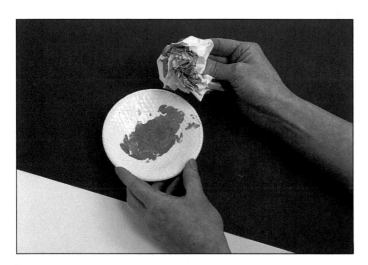

1. Lay the sheet of paper on a flat surface. Pour a small amount of gold paint into a saucer or mixing palette. Take a piece of cloth or tissue paper, about 8 × 8in, and crumple it in your hand. Press the crumpled surface onto the paint in the saucer, taking particular care not to overload the paper or cloth with paint.

2. Press the paint-coated surface onto the paper to create a mottled pattern. Work all over the surface of the paper with a light, dabbing action. Make sure that you do not smudge the paint as you work.

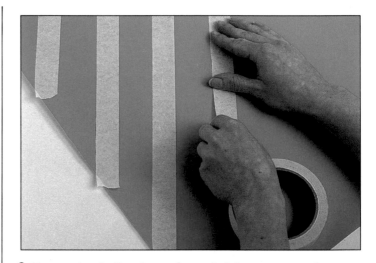

3. For a striped effect, lay a sheet of plain paper on a flat surface. Place masking tape in diagonal stripes, about 1in apart, across it.

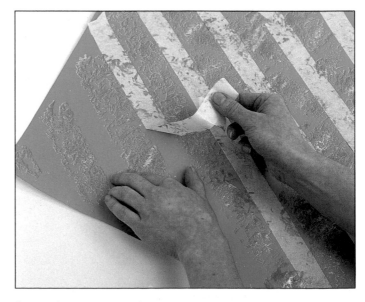

4. Use the mottling technique described in steps 1 and 2 to apply random splodges of gold paint over the surface of the paper. Leave to dry before removing the masking tape.

5. If you prefer checks to stripes, fold a sheet of poster paper concertina style, with each fold about ¾in wide. To protect your work surface cover with newspaper. Stretch out the paper a little on your work top and use a metal gold spray paint to coat the paper with a fine mist of paint. Spray from one angle only, so that one side of each fold catches the paint creating a striped effect when the paper is opened out.

6. When the paint is completely dry, repeat the process, but this time making the folds at right angles to the first folds.

7. Add a special finishing touch to the present with matching gift tags and pretty folded fans.

CHRISTMAS CRACKERS

Crackers are a traditional part of Christmas, but they do not simply have to contain a little plastic trinket and a paper hat. You could put any small gift – no matter how expensive – in the middle of these festive crackers. The first project is simply an alternative way of wrapping a small gift. The second will make your festivities go with a bang!

TARTAN CRACKERS

YOU WILL NEED

Thin card, 9 × 7in
Tartan paper, 13½ × 7in
About 2ft paper lace
Clear, all-purpose adhesive
Double-sided adhesive tape

Fine string or strong thread
Fine-gauge wire
Paper ribbon bows (optional)
Sprigs of heather (optional)

1. Cut the thin card into three pieces, one measuring 7 × 3½in and two measuring 7 × 2¾in. Form the two smaller pieces into tubes. Stick paper lace along the short edges of the tartan paper.

2. Roll the larger piece of card into a tube and place it in the center of the paper. Insert your gift and fasten the paper around the tube, using double-sided tape. Tie the paper with string or thread at the ends of the central tube, then open out the ends and insert the small tubes into the ends.

3. Thread some fine wire through lengths of paper lace and gather it up. Tie it around the joints in the cracker, twisting the wire together firmly to hold it in place. Decorate the cracker with paper ribbon bows and sprigs of heather if wished.

TRADITIONAL CRACKERS

YOU WILL NEED

Tracing paper
White card
Metallic finish crepe paper
  in colors of your choice
Scissors
Pinking shears
Pencil

Double-sided adhesive tape
3 inner tubes from rolls of
  toilet tissue
Cracker snap
Narrow ribbon to match
  paper

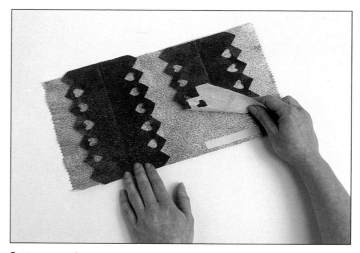

3. Position the contrasting pieces about 1in in from the ends of the larger piece and stick in place with strips of double-sided adhesive tape.

1. Copy the template (page 121) and transfer the outline to a piece of white card. Cut a rectangle, 13½ × 7in, from one of the colors of crepe paper, and two pieces, each 7 × 6¼in, from a contrasting color. Always cut crepe paper so that the grain runs along the length of the cracker. Use pinking shears to trim both ends of the large rectangle. Fold the smaller pieces in half, matching the 7in sides, and place a template to the fold in the paper. Use a pencil to draw all around the template.

4. Trim the cardboard tubes so that one is 4⅛in long and the other two are 2⅛in long. Turn over the crepe paper and place the long tube in the center, with the other two tubes about ½in from the pinked edges. Slip the cracker snap inside the tubes, and place a gift or some wrapped candy in the center tube.

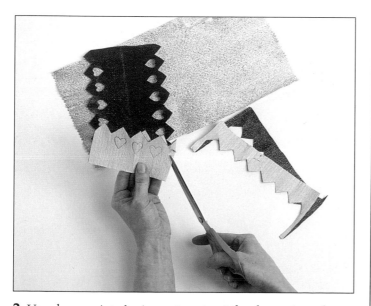

2. Use sharp pointed scissors to cut out the shapes from the smaller rectangles.

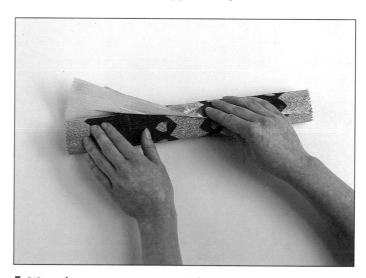

5. Wrap the crepe paper around the tubes, and use double-sided adhesive tape to stick the crepe paper firmly in place.

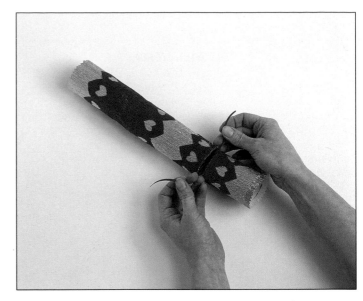

120

6. Hold the center of the cracker in one hand and one end in your other hand. Gently twist the cracker clockwise, then anticlockwise. This creases the paper between the tubes and makes it easier to tie in the next step.

7. Take a short length of matching ribbon and tie the cracker tightly around the creased part. Trim off the ends of the ribbon. Fasten the other end in the same way.

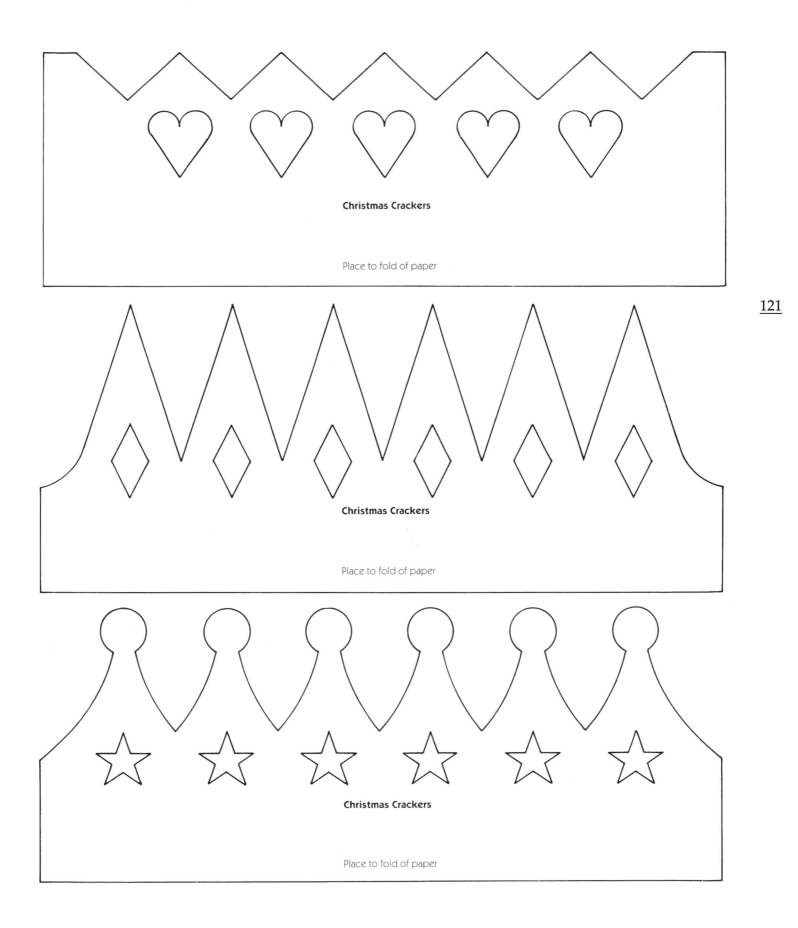

Christmas Crackers

Place to fold of paper

Christmas Crackers

Place to fold of paper

Christmas Crackers

Place to fold of paper

BLUE AND GOLD

When you want to give a present to someone extra special, an elegant and beautiful decoration on a simply wrapped gift can make it unforgettable. The leaves used here are silk, fastened to wire stems. The little baubles and tree decorations have also been wired, while the contrast is provided by little pieces of Finland moss.

YOU WILL NEED

Gold ribbon to tie around
   parcel and make bow
Scissors
Wire cutters
Finland moss

Selection of silk leaves,
   baubles, decorations,
   all wired
Low-melt glue and glue
   pan

122

1. Wrap the parcel and bind it lengthways with gold ribbon, sealing the ends with a spot of glue or double-sided tape.

2. Make a bow, adding four loops to each side, and stick it on the band of gold ribbon, positioning it where the ribbon ends finish to hide the join.

3. Use wire cutters to trim the ends of the wires and glue the leaves into the center of the bow. Add the decorative parcel and gold balls and berries. To finish, dip small pieces of Finland moss in the glue and tuck them well into the design.

FANCY DRESS

Make a plain box a gift in its own right by decorating it to look like something else. Use your imagination to create a costume appropriate to the recipient of the gift, and use any of the paper techniques – pleating, folding, curling, and cutting – to create a truly original wrapping. For a New Year gift, wrapping the gifts in evening dress seemed appropriate.

YOU WILL NEED

Colored and plain white,   Glue stick
  black, and gray papers   Felt-tipped pens
Double-sided tape   Buttons

1. Wrap the box in plain white paper. Cut strips of gray paper about ½in wide.

2. Wrap black paper around the parcel so that it meets at the center front, and turn back the corners for the lapels. Stick the gray stripes along the bottom edge to form the shape of the pocket.

3. Cut out two bow tie shapes and stick them together with a piece of tape. Decorate the tie and stick it in place. Add a flower, buttons, and a label.

BOTTLE WITH A DIFFERENCE

What could be better to welcome in the New Year than a bottle of champagne, and if you are visiting friends or staying with relatives, this decorated bottle would be the perfect gift. The flowers and leaves are silk, and they are attached to the side of the bottle with a small piece of dry floral foam (Oasis), known as a mini-deco. These little semicircular pads are especially designed to allow you to create miniature displays on the sides of bottles or even cakes.

YOU WILL NEED

Oasis mini-deco
Selection of assorted silk
  foliage, including ferns
Bere grass
Silk Christmas roses
Low-melt glue and glue
  pan
Gold bow with wire
Finland moss

126

1. Make sure that the surface of the bottle is absolutely clean. Peel off the circle of backing paper from the mini-deco and press it firmly on the surface of the bottle.

2. Insert small pieces of foliage around the edge of the mini-deco, adding some strands of bere grass around the edge.

3. Dip the ends of the Christmas roses in glue before positioning them. Dip the wire of the bow in the glue and add it in the center of the arrangement. Put a spot of glue on the ends of the bere grass and bend them over toward the center to form loops. Mask any foam that is still visible with clumps of moss.

Easter, Halloween, — and Harvest —

Why use only conventional papers and ribbons when you are wrapping gifts? In this section we concentrate on ideas for using natural materials, not only as a source of inspiration for unusual gift-wrapping ideas but also as the base materials for the wrapping itself.

Seeds, pods, spices, and many fruits dry easily and quickly. They make fragrant and beautiful additions to your gifts (as well as excellent Christmas tree decorations). Fall is the ideal time to begin to prepare fruit and spices so that you have a wealth of material that can be used later in the year and that will keep until spring. A single layer of citrus slices and spices kept in a warm, dry place will be ready to use in three or four weeks. Fresh and dried herbs and spices can be bought in supermarkets and specialist food stores, and you can coordinate this natural look by using green and brown boxes, raffia, and string.

Leaves are a wonderful form of natural decoration. They come in all shapes, sizes, and colors, and, best of all, they are completely free. Collect leaves all year round. Place them between layers of smooth tissue paper, surround them with newspaper, then weight them down with books for about two weeks.

COVERED BOXES

Boxes can be reused. Chocolate and soap boxes are often especially suitable for use with other gifts, and it is often necessary only to cover the top of the lid, but the same method can be used to cover the bottom too.

YOU WILL NEED
Ruler Paper Scissors Glue stick

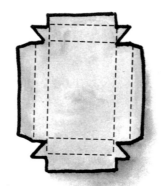

130

1. Measure the width and length of the box lid and the height of the box sides. The piece of paper will have to be large enough for the lid measurement plus four times the sides. Draw the rectangle in the center of a piece of lightweight paper. Add sides all round, and then add another set of sides to turn under. Draw "ears" as shown.

2. Cut out, score, and fold the whole shape. Position the box on the drawn rectangle and turn the "ears" inwards.

3. Stick the "ears" and the turn-in allowance down.

4. Stick down the opposite sides firmly.

LEFT: Interesting patterns can be made from corrugated card. Always cut the card with a sharp knife from the wrong (flat) side, but do not press too hard so that you do not flatten the ribs. Use a fairly strong adhesive. Cover the top first and then, with the covered top downwards, wrap a strip of corrugated paper around the sides.

WOVEN PAPER

Weaving is another simple technique that can be used to great effect, whether you use it for small tags and cards, or for larger things, such as the bag shown here. Use any type of paper you have to hand – newsprint, crepe paper, tissue paper, or even handmade paper. You can achieve a range of effects by weaving only parts of the paper or by using a mixture of colors and widths.

YOU WILL NEED	
Colored paper	Craft knife or scalpel
Scissors	Ruler

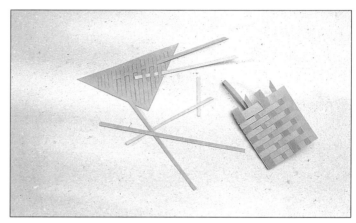

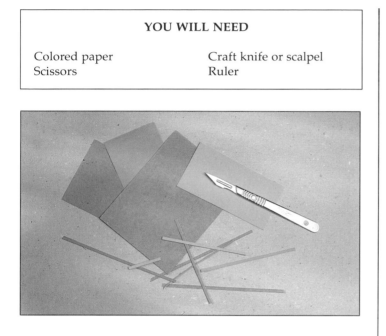

1. Cut some colored paper into the shape of a tag. Cut several narrow strips in contrasting colors for the weaving.

2. Cut a series of regularly spaced slits in the tag. Weave the first strip over and under the slits, then weave the second strip under and over. Leave the ends different lengths, or trim them off neatly.

BELOW: To make the woven newspaper bag, fold some newspaper into strips about ½in and pin a row of strips about ½in apart to a thick piece of cardboard, Weave other strips in and out, alternately, to form a flat sheet. Fold the sheet in half and glue the sides together to make a bag. Tape paper ribbon handles to the top before filling with raffia, eggs, and your gift. Fill natural and colored woven baskets with shredded tissue, straw, and a mixture of hand-painted and chocolate eggs.

FALL LEAVES

You can produce a wide variety of designs using either natural prints or stencils, and the two techniques are combined in this card, which has an attractive leaf motif.

YOU WILL NEED

Leaves (any fairly flat leaves will do)
Paintbrush
Gouache paint: red
Palette or saucer
Sheets of sugar paper, 11½ × 8¼in: red, cream, green

Double-sided adhesive tape
Gold spray
Clear, all-purpose adhesive
Cream card, about 12 × 8in
Fine gold pen

132

1. Choose a suitable leaf, then trim off the stalk if necessary. Paint the underside of the leaf, where the veins are prominent, with red gouache paint.

3. Carefully peel back the top sheet of paper to reveal the print. This process can be repeated several times if you wish.

2. Place the leaf on a sheet of paper with the painted side facing upward. Put another piece over the leaf, and press down. Rub over the area.

4. Select several leaves of the same kind and place them in a random pattern on a sheet of colored paper. Hold them in place with small pieces of adhesive tape. Spray over the leaves, ideally using an old cardboard box to protect your working area. Leave to dry for 5 minutes.

5. When the paint is dry, carefully remove the leaves from the paper.

7. Tear the leaf print to size, using a ruler to help tear a neat edge, and decorate the torn edges with a gold pen.

6. Cut the background to size and glue it to a larger, folded piece of contrasting colored card.

133

8. Glue the leaf print on to the sprayed background to complete the card.

STENCILED LEAVES

The key to stenciling is to use a dry brush, which will not only give the best results but will help the stencil to last longer. Presents wrapped in paper decorated with these natural shapes will look good tied with string, raffia, or paper ribbon, and you can use scraps of decorated paper to add interest to a plainly wrapped parcel.

YOU WILL NEED

Leaves
Medium weight paper
Sharp pointed scissors or
 scalpel

Stencil or gouache paint in
 shades of green
Saucer or palette
Stencil brush

134

1. Choose an interestingly shaped leaf and draw around it on a sheet of medium weight paper. If you intend to reuse the stencil for several sheets, use a more robust material such as acetate.

2. Carefully cut out the leaf. If you want a perfectly symmetrical shape, fold the paper in half and cut both sides together. In nature, though, leaves are more often slightly asymmetric.

3. Mix the paint to a thick consistency and keep the brush as dry as possible. Lay the stencil over the paper and evenly dab on the paint.

Real leaves can be used as templates for cutting shapes out of brown paper to use for tags. Paint or spatter the leaf shapes with gouache or poster paint, or leave them brown. Punch a hole in the tag, and thread through string or raffia and tie to the wrapped present.

SPATTERING

Spattering is a simple decorative technique. You need a selection of gouache or poster paints, paper, and an old toothbrush or stencil brush. The gifts have been wrapped in brown paper that was spattered with paint, they were then tied with raffia and string, and decorated with real leaves and paper cut-outs, spattered with paint. Dried twigs and berries were added for the final embellishment.

YOU WILL NEED

Medium weight paper or acetate
Leaves

Gouache or poster paint
Old toothbrush or stencil brush

136

1. Use a real leaf to make a template from medium weight paper or acetate. Mix the paints to a medium consistency and to produce various shades of green, brown, and gold.

2. Dip the brush into the first color and run your finger across the bristles to produce a fine spray effect. Repeat with other colors. Punch a hole and add a raffia or string tie.

WICKED WITCH

This pop-up design has height and opens with an appropriately large, sweeping movement that will always be remembered. The construction is simple, but the stick supporting the witch must be strong, and the V-angle that it forms at the base must be carefully adjusted so that the witch collapses into the front corner of the card. The grid is drawn to a scale of 1:2½.

YOU WILL NEED

Backing sheet (thin blue card glued to mounting card), 15¼ × 8½in
Adhesive tape
Thin blue card (for support), about 8 × 2½in
Scissors

Thick black paper (for witch), about 6 × 6in
Medium weight white paper (for clouds), about 6 × 6in
Craft knife or scalpel
Clear, all-purpose adhesive

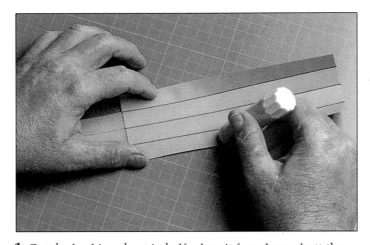

1. Cut the backing sheet in half, place it face down, butt the cut edges together, and stick them together with tape so that it will lie flat after being folded. Use the template (LEFT) to cut out the pieces. Apply glue to the outer, long panels of the support, then fold them inward so that they align with the center crease, halving the width, and doubling the thickness of the support.

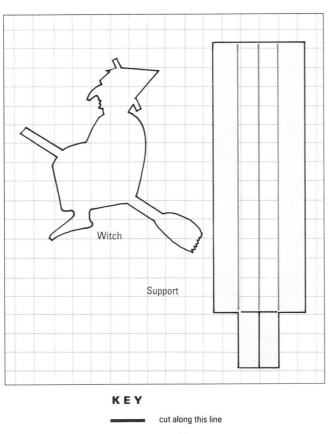

Witch

Support

KEY

— cut along this line

— mountain crease

— valley crease

▢ glue here (sometimes on the underside)

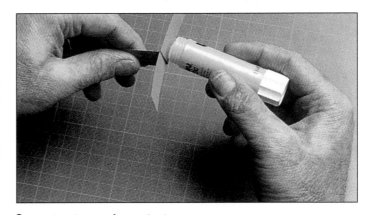

2. Apply glue to the end tabs.

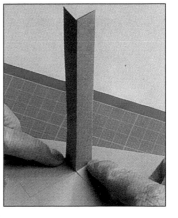

3. Glue the tabs to the backing sheet.

4. Glue the witch to the top of the stick.

5. If the angle of the fold in step 3 is carefully judged, the witch will collapse into the front corner of the backing sheet when the card is shut.

138

FLAT-GIFT HOLDER

This type of box is most suitable for gifts such as scarves and ties, which need to be folded neatly and kept flat. The boxes can be decorated in a variety of ways.

Measure the gift, then make the holder the length of the gift. If the gift is solid, allow a little extra. At its deepest point, the curves at the top and bottom of the holder should measure approximately twice the height of the gift.

With these measurements, it is now possible to draw the plan of the gift holder (see diagram). The curve can either be drawn with compasses, placed on the center line, or by using a dinner plate of a suitable size. Join two sides with one curve, and trace this off on a piece of scrap card. Use this as a template to draw the other curves. Cut out and score the card. Stick the glue flap to the side. Place the gift in the holder and close by turning in the curves.

BELOW: The blue gift holder is decorated with a cut-out butterfly shape. The green one was made with lightweight card that was decorated with a stenciled design.

PYRAMID BOX

This little box can either be used to contain a gift or as decoration on it – the size can be varied as you wish depending on the gift that you have to wrap.

YOU WILL NEED

Sheet of card	Ruler
Pencil	Glue stick
Pair of compasses	Craft knife/scalpel

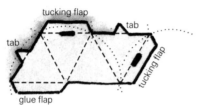

1. Draw a line the length of the base of one side. Draw a semicircle on the line. Place the compass point, with the same radius, at one end of the semicircle and mark the center and the point it crosses on the curve.

2. Repeat from the other end of the line.

3. With the same radius setting, draw another semicircle so that it joins the first.

4. Put the compass point on the join and mark the point it crosses on this curve. Join all the marks, and you will have four equilateral triangles.

5. Add a glue flap to the base of the first triangle, two tucking flaps with slits, and two tabs to correspond to the slits.

6. Cut out the basic shape and score all the other lines.

7. Stick the glue flap and place the gift inside and close the box tightly with the tabs. Although it is tricky to tuck in the tabs, they do give a very secure closure.

You can make a pyramid box that is any size. Use plain or foiled card, or decorate plain card with stencils or by spattering.

SEE-THROUGH SOLUTION

Here is a pretty and practical solution to the perennial problem of wrapping a spherical gift.

YOU WILL NEED

Tissue paper
Fine string or strong
  thread
Cellophane or acetate
Craft ribbon

1. Place the gift on a large square of brightly colored tissue paper. Bring the edges to the top.

2. Tie tightly with a piece of strong thread, and spread out the bunched-up paper at the top.

3. Cover the wrapped gift in the same way, but this time with crisp acetate or cellophane. Tie it with another piece of thread.

4. Finish off with a bright length of ribbon in a contrasting color and tie a neat bow. Alternatively, add a tassel or attach some beads to some colored cord.

MESSAGE IN THE BOTTLE

A corrugated cardboard tube is an excellent way of wrapping a bottle and it can look surprisingly decorative. Use plain or colored, stiff, corrugated cardboard or any thick, bendable card.

YOU WILL NEED

Corrugated cardboard
Craft knife or scissors
Strong adhesive or
  double-sided adhesive
  tape
Plain card
Narrow ribbon to decorate

1. Measure the circumference and height of the bottle and cut the cardboard so that it is a little taller than the bottle and will wrap around it, overlapping by about ¼in.

2. Glue or use double-sided tape to stick the sides of the cardboard together to make a tube.

3. Cut out a round piece of thick, non-corrugated card for the base and glue it to the bottom of the tube. You may find it easier to make four small tabs of thin card, which you can use to attach the base to the tube.

4. Cut a piece of corrugated cardboard for the lid. It should fit tightly over the main tube but be loose enough to slide on easily. Glue or tape the edges together to form a tube.

5. Cut a second circle from thick, non-corrugated card for the top of the lid and glue or tape it in place.

6. Put the bottle inside the tube, slide on the lid, and tie securely with narrow ribbon.

GOOD LUCK AND
— CONGRATULATIONS —

In this section are some ideas for those occasions when you want to give someone a little gift to wish them well or send a card to show that you are thinking of them. Moving house, for example, is one of the most stressful things that a family can do, so how better to welcome your friends or relatives to their new home than by sending a handmade card or a thoughtfully packaged little gift?

Cover empty chocolate or tea-bag boxes with shop-bought gift-wrap, or cover your presents with colorful tissue paper. Decorate the gifts with shredded paper for a colorful and unusual alternative to a ribbon bow. Experiment with cellophane, which can be used to cover plain, bright colors, giving an extra sparkle and sheen to a brilliant primary shade, and look out for patterned cellophane, which is available with colorful spots and squiggles over the surface.

WAX RESIST CARD

This is an ideal technique for children, and it works especially well with fairly simple motifs such as flowers, hearts, and animals. It has been used here to make a card to welcome someone to a new home.

YOU WILL NEED

White wax crayon or candle
Watercolor paper
Paintbrushes
Gouache paints: orange, red, yellow

Clear, all-purpose adhesive or double-sided adhesive tape
Colored card, 12 × 5in
Scissors

144

1. Draw the design on watercolor paper using a candle or white wax crayon. If you tilt the paper slightly in the light you can see the lines you have drawn.

2. Take a brush loaded with paint and apply it to the paper. For best results, limit the number of colors you use, although it is possible to mix them on the paper to get different shades.

3. Blend the paints together on the paper with a clean brush and water. Leave to dry for 10–20 minutes.

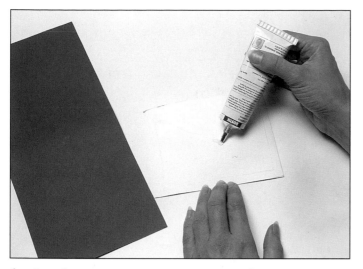

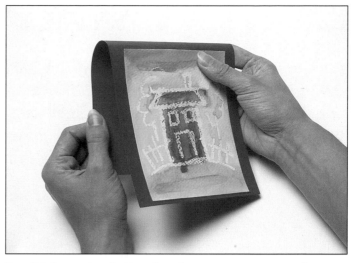

4. When the paint is completely dry, use adhesive or double-sided tape to stick the design to the large piece of contrasting colored card.

5. Fold the card in half so that the image appears on the front of the card.

START PACKING

A design such as this can be varied in as many ways as you want – you can design it to suit a particular family, perhaps by including a piano, or some favorite toys or pieces of furniture, or a pet dog. If you use this pattern, add some humorous labels to the boxes. Often, the more a card is personalized – and the less like a shop-bought card it looks – the more it is appreciated. The grid is drawn to a scale of 1:2½.

YOU WILL NEED

Backing sheet (thin mottled brown card), 11 × 8¾in	Thin mottled brown card (for supports and packing cases), about 18 × 8in	Scissors
Adhesive tape		Fine black felt-tipped pen
		Craft knife or scalpel
		Clear, all-purpose adhesive

146

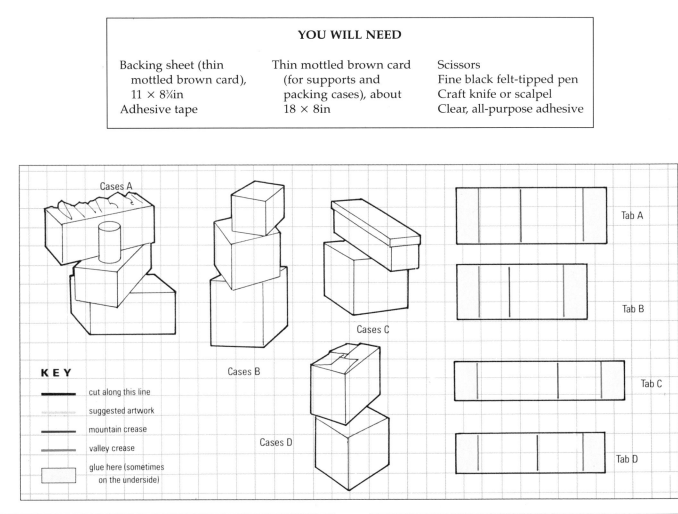

KEY

— cut along this line

· · · suggested artwork

— mountain crease

— valley crease

☐ glue here (sometimes on the underside)

Cases A
Cases B
Cases C
Cases D

Tab A
Tab B
Tab C
Tab D

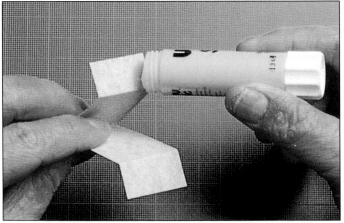

1. Cut the backing sheet in half, place it face down, butt the cut edges together, and stick them together with tape so that it will lie flat after being folded. Use the template (Above) to cut out the pieces. Apply glue to both ends of tab A.

2. Position it at the left of the backing sheet.

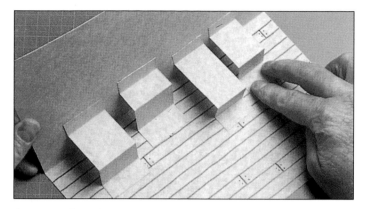

3. Apply the other tabs in the same way, checking the alignment of each.

5. Repeat step 4 for cases B, C, and D.

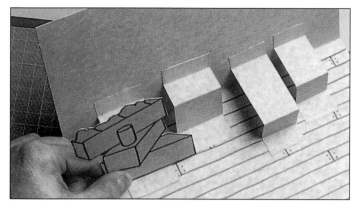

4. Glue packing case A onto tab A.

147

6. Redraw the black lines of the tabs.

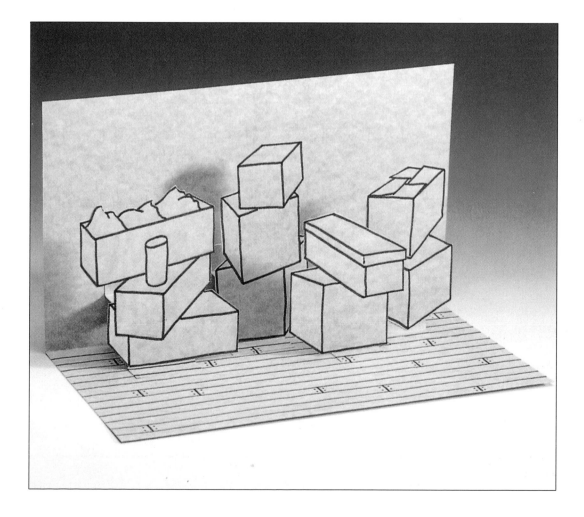

FUN REMOVALS

The van in this design is a modified box, but the pop-up element lies parallel to the backing sheet, not at an angle. Using this adaptable technique, a whole fleet of vehicles could be constructed, as well as boats, ships, and airplanes. The sides of the van can be enlivened by adding an apposite name. The grid is drawn to a scale of 1:2.

KEY

▬▬▬	cut along this line
▬▬▬	suggested artwork
▬▬▬	mountain crease
▬▬▬	valley crease
▭	glue here (sometimes on the underside)
⊢——⊣	these measurements are the same

YOU WILL NEED

Backing sheet (thin pink
  card glued to mounting
  card), 8¾ × 6½in
Adhesive tape
Scissors

Thin green card (for van),
  about 14 × 6in
Craft knife or scalpel
Clear, all-purpose adhesive

148

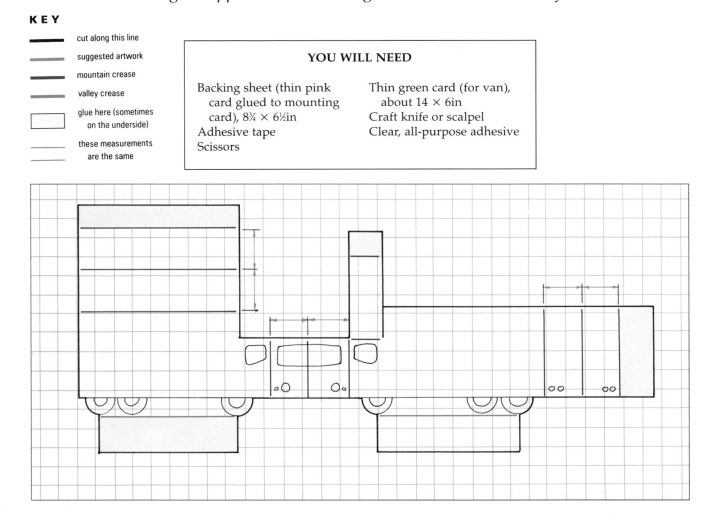

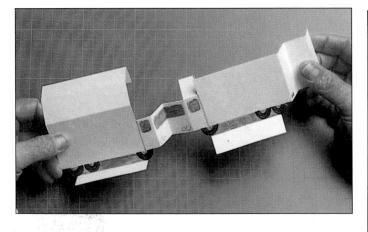

1. Cut the backing sheet in half, place it face down, butt the cut edges together, and stick them together with tape so that it will lie flat after being folded. Use the template (ABOVE) to cut out the van. Make all the creases.

2. Apply glue to the end tab and glue it into the vehicle.

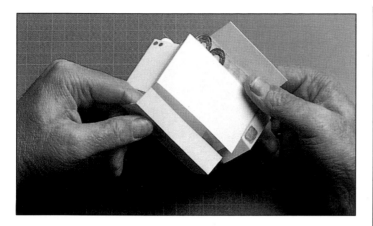

3. Glue in the two top tabs.

5. Push the tabs through the slits and tape them flat to the reverse of the backing sheet.

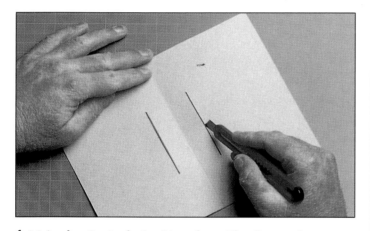

4. Make the slits in the backing sheet. The distance between them is the width of the van.

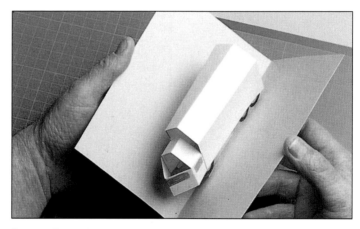

6. Note how the vehicle opens and flattens when the card is folded flat.

NEW HOME, SWEET HOME

This is a complicated card to make, but it looks so good that you will want to try it if you have successfully attempted any of the other pop-up designs in this book. The house is made in the form of a box, as is the fence. The telegraph pole is attached to the fence, and the chimney is not attached to the roof, but to the backing sheet, which increases the three-dimensional effect. The grid is drawn to a scale of 1:2½.

YOU WILL NEED

Backing sheet (white mounting card), 12 × 8¾in
Adhesive tape
Thin green, brown, dark green, gray, and white card (for all other pieces), about 12 × 10in in total
Scissors
Craft knife or scalpel
Clear, all-purpose adhesive
Masking tape

KEY

───── cut along this line
───── suggested artwork
───── mountain crease
───── valley crease
▭ glue here (sometimes on the underside)

150

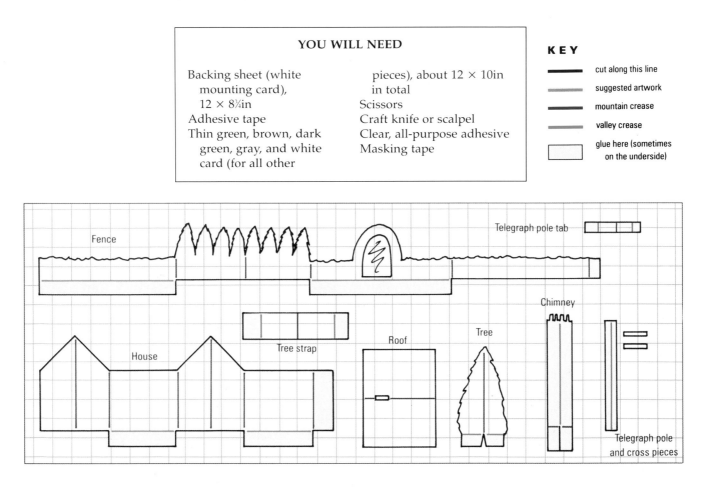

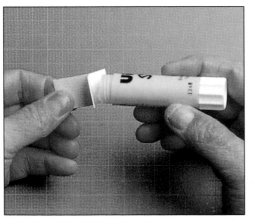

1. Cut the backing sheet in half, place it face down, butt the cut edges together, and stick them together with tape so that it will lie flat after being folded. Use the template (ABOVE) to cut out the pieces. Apply glue to both ends of the tree strap.

2. Glue the strap across the central crease on the backing sheet. The strap folds up when the card is closed.

3. Glue the tree to one end of the strap.

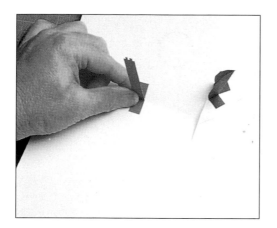

4. Glue and fold the chimney so that it is double thickness, and glue its tabs to the backing sheet, each side of the central crease.

5. Glue the tab at the end of the house to the other end to make it three-dimensional.

6. Add masking tape to the long top edges of the house, then lower on the roof. Fix it in place so that it rests in the correct position. This may take several attempts, and you will need to open out the house to check that you have got it right.

7. Apply glue to the underside of the house tabs.

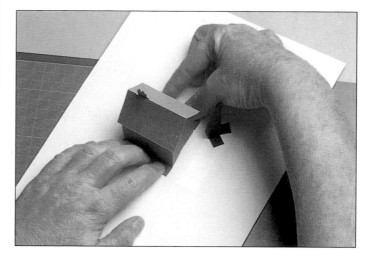

8. Glue them to the backing sheet, taking care to lower the house over the chimney and to pull the house fully open.

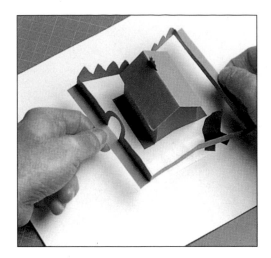

9. Similarly, fold and glue the fence to the backing sheet. Stretch it so that it is square.

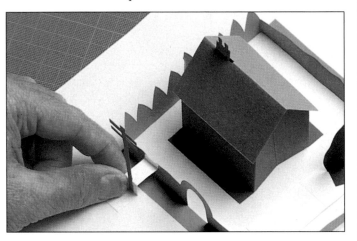

10. Glue the telegraph pole to the fence and backing sheet. Assemble the telegraph pole and cross-pieces and glue to the front of the tab.

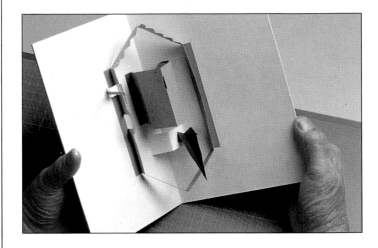

11. When the card is closed, all the separate pieces collapse.

HEXAGONAL BOX

This box looks most impressive, but it is not as complicated to make as it appears. Once the size of the hexagon has been decided upon, it is quite easy to construct. If the box is being used for a circular gift, make sure that this fits within the hexagon.

YOU WILL NEED

Sheet of card
Pair of compasses
Pencil
Ruler
Scissors
Glue stick

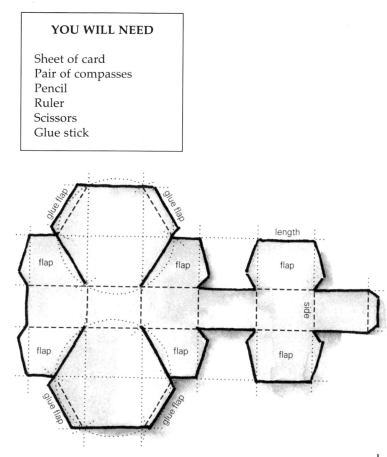

BELOW: This hexagonal box was made using embossed foil card. Filled with foil-wrapped chocolates, it makes an impressive gift.

153

1. Draw a circle larger than the gift. Draw a horizontal line through the center of the circle.

2. Using the same radius setting, place the compass point on one of the intersections and mark the point it crosses on the curve.

3. Move the compass to this point, and repeat until you have six points around the circumference.

4. Join these points and check again that the gift will fit in the base of the box. Then draw a plan, using the diagram as a guide.

5. The sides of the box are equal to the height of the gift and one side of the hexagon in length. The three flaps, top and bottom, are half the height of the hexagon.

6. Cut out and score the box. Fold the pieces. Check the angles before gluing the flaps in case any adjustments are necessary.

7. Stick the glue flap and assemble the box. If necessary, stick down the tucking flaps on the base so that the box does not fall apart if the gift is heavy.

BROWN PAPER CARDS

This technique was discovered while experimenting with inks and brown parcel paper. You can use it to produce one-off pictures or make color copies of your originals to create multiple versions of the same design. This card shown in the project has a baby motif, and it could be used to celebrate the birth of a child.

YOU WILL NEED

Pencil
Brown parcel paper,
  3 × 3in
Fine felt-tipped pen
Black water-soluble
  marker pen
Garden water spray
Gold marker pen
Cream card, 8 × 6in
Clear, all-purpose
  adhesive

1. Draw the design in pencil on the brown paper, tracing the template here if you are not confident of your artistic skills. Go over the lines with a fine black pen.

3. Use a water spray to mist over the picture with water. The image will "bleed" around the edges. Dab off any excess water with a paper towel, then leave to dry for about 20 minutes.

4. Add any further decoration with a gold marker pen.

2. Draw a frame around the design, then fill in the area between the frame and the design with a black water-soluble marker pen.

5. Trim to size, then glue directly to the front of a folded piece of cream card.

PRESENT PERFECT

Pop-up boxes are especially pleasing to make because, unlike other techniques, they fully enclose a space to create a real sense of volume. The lid pieces need to be accurately cut so that the top closes fully. The grid is drawn to a scale of 1:2.

YOU WILL NEED

Backing sheet (thin
    textured gray card
    glued to mounting
    card), 11 × 6½in
Adhesive tape
Thick yellow and red card
    (for box and ribbons), a
    total of about 12 × 6in
Scissors
Craft knife or scalpel
Clear, all-purpose
    adhesive

KEY

——— cut along this line

═══ mountain crease

▭ glue here (sometimes
    on the underside)

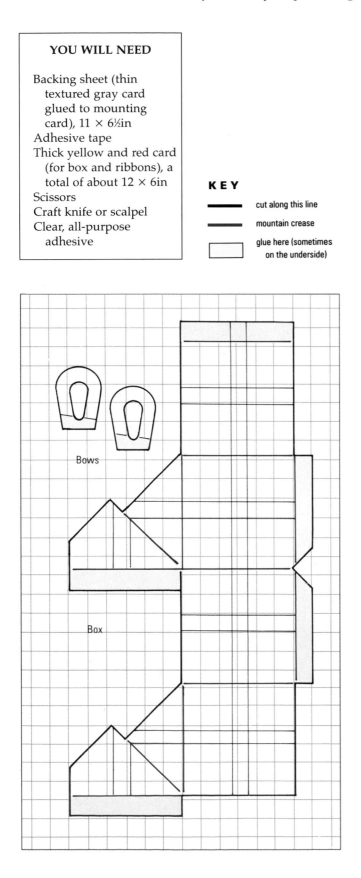

Bows

Box

1. Cut the backing sheet in half, place it face down, butt the cut edges together, and stick them together with tape so that it will lie flat after being folded. Use the template (LEFT) to cut out the box and ribbons. Apply glue to the underside of the bows, position them on the box and glue them in place.

2. Crease the box as shown and add glue to the end tab.

3. Fold and make a square tube.

4. Apply glue to each lid tab in turn. The photograph shows the outer face of a tab being glued, so that the tab lies inside the box. However, if the inner face is glued, so that the tab lies outside the box, the pop-up has more strength and will not burst. The disadvantage is that the tab will be seen. So decide which is best for your card.

6. Glue the box to the backing sheet.

157

5. Glue the underside of the tabs at the base of the box. Note that the tabs are folded inwards.

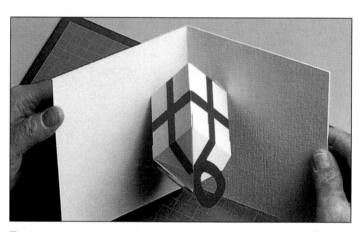

7. This shows how the pop-up box closes. Note how the lid pieces separate.

A SLICE OF CAKE

If you use reflective card for the backing sheet, the completed card will make it look as if there are several slices of cake. The folds must be accurately marked and creased if the card is to open smoothly. The grid is drawn to a scale of 1:2.

YOU WILL NEED

Backing sheet (thick mirror card), 10¼ × 6½in
Adhesive tape
Thin white card (for cake), 8 × 6in
Felt-tipped pens
Scissors
Craft knife or scalpel
Clear, all-purpose adhesive

1. Cut the backing sheet in half, place it face down, butt the cut edges together, and stick them together with tape so that it will lie flat after being folded. Use the template (BELOW) to cut out the cake. Cut two slits in the backing sheet.

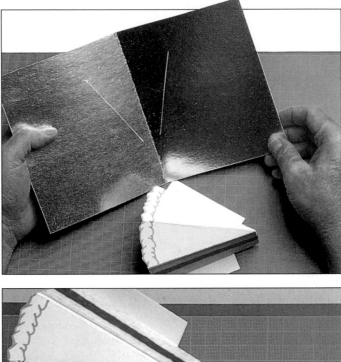

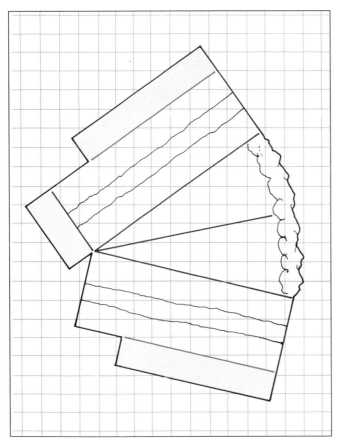

2. Fold the decorated cake along the lines and glue the tab on the point of the cake wedge to make the cake three-dimensional.

3. Push the tabs along the bottom of the cake through the slits in the backing sheet.

KEY

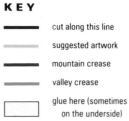

cut along this line

suggested artwork

mountain crease

valley crease

glue here (sometimes on the underside)

4. They should fit through them like this.

5. Use adhesive tape to hold the tabs flat on the reverse of the backing sheet.

6. The cake complete. Reflective card will make this slice of cake appear to be many.

INDIAN IDEAS

Presents to celebrate a special occasion often call for something a little out of the ordinary, and here are some ideas based on the vibrant colors and intricate decorations of India. Some specialist stores stock exquisite silks, ribbons, and accessories, and you should also look out for tassels, little fabric birds, and metal ornaments.

Marbled papers are widely available, but you can easily make your own version at home. Simply fill a large plastic dish, about 2½in deep, with thin wallpaper paste. Mix two or three colors of oil paint with mineral (white) spirit until they are of a medium consistency. Drop spots of color on the paste and gently stir with a knitting needle. Place the paper carefully on the surface of the oil, lift it out, and leave to dry.

More in keeping with the exotic theme, however, are glowing foils and metallic papers, colored silk tassels, and little metal charms and trinkets. These irresistible parcels are finished off with rather unusual tags.

160

YOU WILL NEED

Medium weight paper	Sequins
Scissors	Clear, all-purpose adhesive
Selection of candy	Ribbon or sewing thread
wrappers	

2. Use adhesive to cover the tag with small, torn pieces of candy wrappers and sequins.

1. Cut out from the paper the shape of the tag. Do not just use rectangles or squares – these tags can be any shape you want.

3. Trim away the excess from around the edges of the tag and punch a hole in the top. Thread through some fine ribbon or several strands of colorful cotton.

RIGHT: *You will find a wide selection of ornaments and tags for decorating your Indian-style gifts. The colored paper labels were, in fact, made from candy wrappers, but the other ornaments were sold as Christmas decorations.*

ABOVE: *When you have wrapped your gift in a single, bright color, tie it with metallic or brightly colored silk ribbons, and add some tassels or little fabric birds.*

ABOVE: *Wrap a narrow strip of hand-marbled paper around a bought paper bag and decorate it with beads and metal charms, threaded on lengths of cotton.*

VALENTINE'S DAY

The heart is a symbol of love and friendship. Heart images can be used on gifts for many different occasions – Mother's Day, a wedding, a christening, and so on – but most often on Valentine's Day. Hearts can be very decorative or simple, symmetrical, or more stylized. On the following pages are some inspirational ideas, ranging from a simple heart-shaped box with a handmade tag to wire hearts threaded with flowers. Look out for old, heart-shaped boxes and containers that can be repainted and decorated.

HEART-SHAPED BAG

This decorative heart-shaped bag is deceptively simple to make. The design is based on a semicircle, and it can be made from many different types of paper or card. It is easy to alter the size – just make sure that the angles are the same as those shown.

YOU WILL NEED

Sheet of card or paper
Pair of compasses
Pencil
Ruler
Protractor
Scissors
Glue stick

164

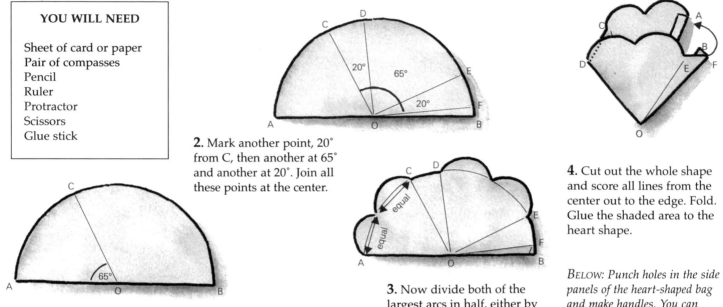

2. Mark another point, 20° from C, then another at 65° and another at 20°. Join all these points at the center.

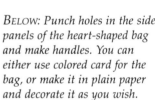

1. Draw a semicircle and make a point about 65° from one edge (C).

3. Now divide both of the largest arcs in half, either by measuring or using a protractor. Draw semicircles on each half.

4. Cut out the whole shape and score all lines from the center out to the edge. Fold. Glue the shaded area to the heart shape.

BELOW: Punch holes in the side panels of the heart-shaped bag and make handles. You can either use colored card for the bag, or make it in plain paper and decorate it as you wish.

GINGERBREAD

They say that the way to the heart is through the stomach, so these gingerbread figures are an unusual but appropriate addition to these little gift bags. Use dried cranberries, bay leaves, and chiles for extra decorations. The red bag has been decorated with a large paper bow, with the bay leaves, raffia, and gingerbread, while chiles and bay leaves have been added to the purple and light brown bag. An easy alternative would be to thread dried cranberries onto some wire, which could then be bent into a heart shape and tied to the gingerbread.

YOU WILL NEED

⅓ cup soft brown sugar
2 tbsp corn syrup
1 tbsp molasses
2 tbsp water
½ cup butter

½ tsp baking soda
1 cup all-purpose flour
1 tsp ground ginger
1 tsp cinnamon

---

1. Bring the sugar, syrup, molasses, and water to a boil, stirring well.

2. Remove the pan from the heat and stir in the butter and baking soda. Stir in the flour and spices, and mix together well.

3. Leave the dough for 1 hour. Pre-heat the oven to 350°F. Roll out the dough on a floured board until it is about ⅛in thick. Cut out the gingerbread shapes and lay on a buttered baking tray.

4. Bake for 10–12 minutes. Pierce holes for hanging while the gingerbread is still warm, and leave to cool on a wire tray.

165

FABRIC COLLAGE

Red hearts are an obvious choice for a Valentine's Day card when you want to show someone how much you care. This easy-to-make card uses scraps of fabric, in shades of pink, red, and orange, and the gold has been added to give a rich, luxurious effect.

YOU WILL NEED

White sugar paper
Pencil
Scissors
Small pieces of red and
   pink felt fabric, about
   6 × 6in
Cotton wool or wadding

Needle and sewing threads
   to match fabrics
Gold and woven patterned
   fabrics
Clear, all-purpose adhesive
White card, about 8 × 6in

166

1. Draw a heart shape on a piece of paper and use it as a template. Cut a heart shape from a piece of pink felt.

2. Place the heart on a background fabric of a different color and stitch it in place with a simple running stitch. Do not sew all the way round the heart, but leave a gap of about ¾in.

3. Push a small amount of cotton wool through the gap to pad the heart, then sew up the opening. This will give the heart a slightly three-dimensional effect.

4. Select a larger piece of a contrasting fabric to back the felt to which the heart is stitched. Cut it to size and stitch them together.

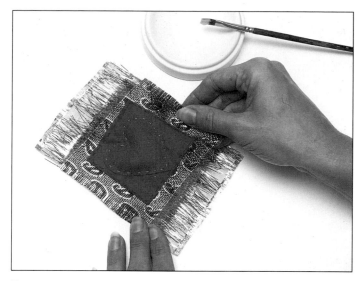

5. If you are using a fine fabric, like the gold one shown, carefully fray the edges to give a decorative effect. As a border, repeat the felt used for the heart. Cut the fabric to size and glue it to the frayed fabric.

6. Glue the whole collage to a larger piece of felt to form a background. Leave to dry for 50–60 minutes.

7. When the glue is dry, glue the completed collage to a larger, contrasting piece of folded card.

FLOWERS AND LEAVES

It has become customary to exchange cards on Valentine's Day, and giving a card that you have made yourself makes the gesture even more personal. Use the flowers and leaves from your garden or from the hedgerows to make your Valentine's card by pressing them, backing them with thin card, then mounting them on colored, fine-corrugated card. Ivy leaves form a charming and natural heart shape – a single leaf could have a little heart cut from it or you could arrange a group of leaves into a pretty heart. Pansies are the symbols of thoughts, and are the most appropriate of flowers to indicate that you are thinking of someone.

YOU WILL NEED

Fresh pansies and ivy
  leaves
Flower press
Colored corrugated card
Craft knife
Double-sided adhesive
  tape
PVA adhesive
Plain paper
Sharp scissors
Adhesive pads (optional)

At least two weeks before you want to make the cards, press the flowers so that they have time to dry thoroughly. Use a flower press or put the flowers and leaves between pieces of tissue paper and place them inside a telephone directory. Place a weight on top and leave completely undisturbed in a warm, dry place for at least 10 days.

2. To make the pansy ring or the heart of ivy leaves, glue the pressed flowers or leaves to plain paper in the arrangement of your choice. When the adhesive is dry, use a craft knife or sharp pointed scissors to cut around the shapes. Attach the cut-out shape to the front of the card with adhesive or, if you want a slightly three-dimensional effect, with adhesive pads.

1. To make the ivy leaf card, take a rectangle of corrugated card, and fold it in half. Cut out a square window in the front. Use double-sided tape or adhesive to glue the paper behind the window. Glue the leaf to the paper, and use a craft knife to cut out a tiny heart in the leaf and then cut around the leaf so that the plain paper falls away. Remember that sections of the leaf must be attached to the card frame on all sides.

CUPID'S ARROW

There is a certain elegance when a supporting tab becomes part of the design of a pop-up card. In this case, the tab that supports the heart has become the arrow. Thus, no part of the design is superfluous. Note also how the arrow slides through the heart when the card is opened. The technique of piercing one pop-up shape with another need not be confined to a large shape and a thin one. Any shape can pierce another, thus eliminating the need for extra supporting tabs. The grid is drawn to a scale of 1:2.

YOU WILL NEED

Backing sheet (thin glossy
  yellow card), 14 × 4½in
Thin red card (for heart),
  5 × 5in
Thin blue card (for arrow),
  6 × 1½in
Scalpel
Clear, all-purpose
  adhesive

170

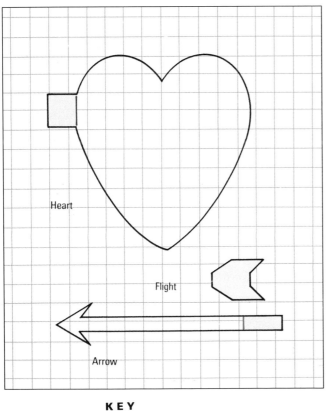

Heart

Flight

Arrow

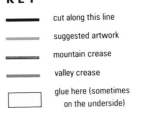

KEY

————— cut along this line

· · · · · · suggested artwork

– – – – – mountain crease

————— valley crease

[ ] glue here (sometimes
  on the underside)

1. Cut the backing sheet in half, place it face down, butt the cut edges together, and stick with tape so that they will lie flat after being folded. Cut out the pieces, using the template (LEFT). Apply glue to the heart tab.

2. Glue the tab to the backing sheet so that the crease in the backing sheet lies approximately behind the center line of the heart.

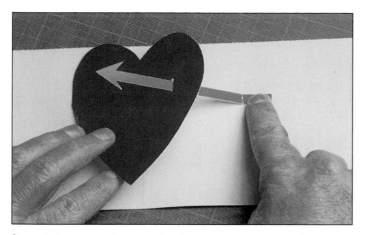

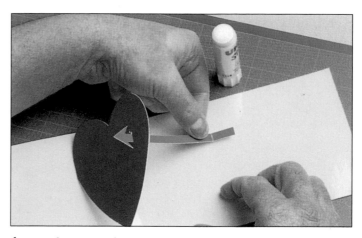

3. Feed the arrow through the slit in the heart from right to left.

4. Glue the end of the arrow to the backing sheet.

5. Glue the flight to the end of the arrow.

TRUE LOVE

This is one of the simplest pop-up cards you could make. Note how the paper is folded behind to create a double thickness that prevents the design from buckling. This also means that the design can be made from paper, rather than card. The grid is drawn to a scale of 1:2½.

YOU WILL NEED

Medium weight red paper,
10¼ × 8in
Scalpel

172

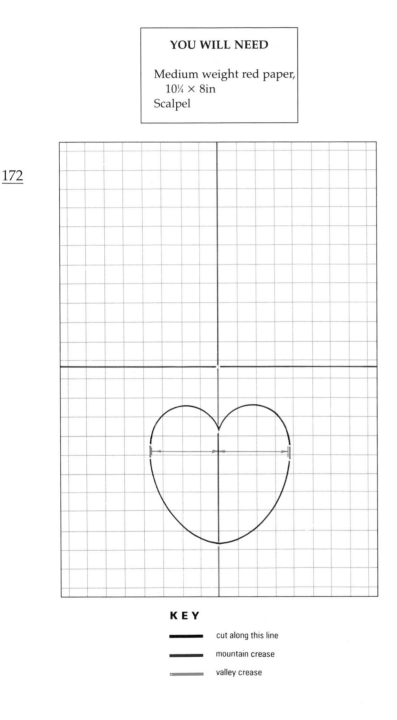

KEY

——— cut along this line

——— mountain crease

——— valley crease

1. Draw half of the heart shape as shown, onto the paper. Fold the sheet in half, not through the heart. Then fold it in half again.

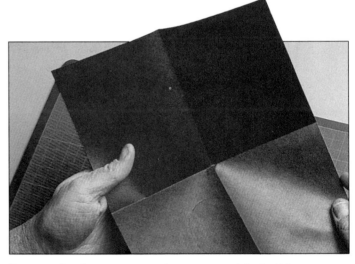

2. Open the sheet out. Note the position of the half-heart.

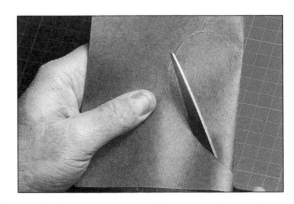

3. Cut out the heart, being careful to leave the small sections uncut that are marked to be folded on the template.

4. Fold back the heart to create these creases.

5. Reform the folds, and pull up the hearts, creating a mountain fold down the center of the heart.

173

Dress up some simple boxes with a few personal touches. Decorate plain ribbon with fabric relief paint and make your own tags. Cut out a large heart outline and a smaller pierced heart, and tie them on with raffia.

HEARTS HAVE IT

Decorate a large sheet of paper with a simple pattern of stenciled hearts – nothing could be simpler, and you can make a gift tag to match and finish it off with some pretty curls of ribbon. Do not worry if the stenciled images do not fit perfectly within the edges of the paper. When you wrap up your gift, you may end up cutting off some of the design.

YOU WILL NEED

Scrap paper
Ruler and pencil
Heart-shaped stencil
Acrylic or stencil paint
Saucer or palette
Stencil brush
Large sheet of red poster
    paper

174

3. When you are happy with the arrangement, plot the same grid on the poster paper. Use very light pencil dots – they should be just dark enough for you to see them as a guide for positioning the stencil but not so dark that they will detract from your design.

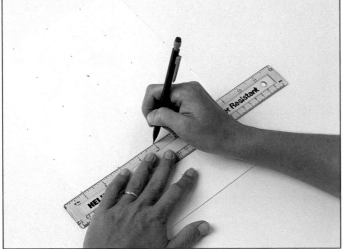

1. On a piece of scrap paper, work out several versions of a grid so that the hearts will be evenly spaced over the paper.

2. Try out a variety of arrangements, spacing the hearts in diagonal patterns or straight lines.

4. Position the stencil on the grid and trace the points of the paper grid onto the stencil using a pencil or permanent marker. This will make it easy for you to position the stencil accurately every time by simply matching the dots.

5. Now stencil the wrapping paper. Make sure that the brush is absolutely clean before you begin, and remember to remove excess paint on a paper towel.

6. As you work, try to make sure that the images are all more or less the same density. Do not try to match them perfectly, however, because the slight differences add to the charm.

175

LEFT: *Make some original gift-wrap paper by stenciling white hearts onto some shop-bought red paper. Make a matching red and white tag, and tie the parcel with white paper ribbon. For a special treat, add a chocolate heart.*

PIERCED PAPER

The technique of piercing paper can be used for gift wrap, tags, ribbons, and cards. The delicate effect is achieved by piercing the paper with the fine point of a needle or nail. Although hearts have been used here, any simple motif would be equally effective.

YOU WILL NEED

Acetate or oiled parchment
   for stencils
Scalpel

Colored paper:
   2 contrasting shades
Needles: 2 different sizes

176

1. Prepare stencils for two hearts, making them different sizes. Cut out a heart of each size from the colored paper.

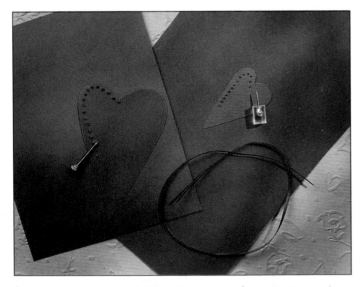

2. Lay the hearts on a soft blanket or something similar, and pierce around the edge of the larger heart with the thicker point.

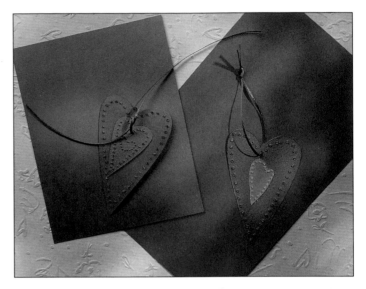

3. Repeat the process with the smaller heart and finer needle. Pierce a hole through the top of each heart, and thread through a ribbon.

ABOVE: Wrap boxes in corrugated card and decorate with pierced paper, ribbon, and tags. Glue some small hearts to pieces of wire and gather them into a bunch to decorate a gift.

PLEATED PAPER

Pleating is a versatile but simple technique, and sections of pleated paper make wonderful gift wraps. Use lightweight paper that can be easily folded. Vary the depths of the pleats and the width of the paper to get different effects, but keep the pleats even and the creases sharp. White, textured, handmade papers look particularly effective. The delicate pleating used on these gifts is reminiscent of Japanese papercraft.

YOU WILL NEED

Sufficient paper to wrap
  the gift plus a piece
  twice the length of the
  parcel
Double-sided adhesive
  tape

1. Cut a piece of paper about twice the length of the wrapped box. Begin folding over the width of the pleat you require. Make a narrow strip of pleated paper and a very small section for the matching tag.

2. Secure the wide piece of pleated paper at one end. Gently twist the paper until the desired effect is achieved, then stick down the other end. Add the narrower pleated strip in the same way.

— MOTHER'S DAY —

The art of wrapping and the art of giving could be said to be one and the same. A beautifully wrapped box shows that you have chosen and wrapped the gift it contains with equal care.

Remember to always choose your wrapping paper with care and to fold it neatly, using double-sided tape to ensure neat edges.

The decorative ribbons you use should start and end at the point where the join will be hidden under a bow or a gift tag. A carefully selected ribbon can turn a plainly wrapped parcel into an attractively wrapped present, while a pretty bow, perhaps combined with silk or ribbon flowers, will transform it into a sensational gift.

SAY IT WITH FLOWERS

This is a simple design in technical terms, but it is very decoratively versatile. The specific shapes of the vase, foliage, and blooms can be varied as you prefer — try roses, tulips, or pansies. The colors shown here are, of course, only suggestions.
The grid is drawn to a scale of 1:2½.

YOU WILL NEED

Backing sheet (white mounting card), 19 × 9in
Double-sided adhesive tape
Thick watercolor paper

(for flowers and vase), 18 × 10in
Scalpel
Felt-tipped pens
Clear, all-purpose adhesive

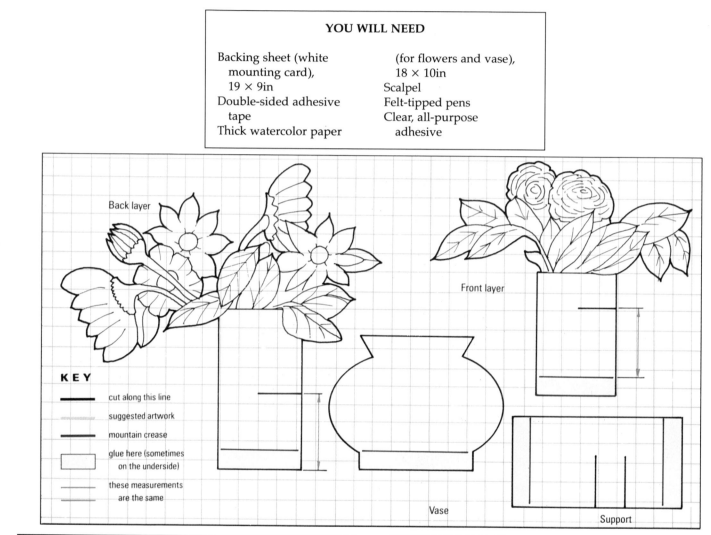

Back layer

Front layer

KEY

cut along this line

suggested artwork

mountain crease

glue here (sometimes on the underside)

these measurements are the same

Vase

Support

1. Cut the backing sheet in half, place it face down, butt the cut edges together, and stick them together with tape so that it will lie flat after being folded. Cut out the pieces.

2. Apply glue to the right-hand edge of the support and glue it to the backing sheet.

3. Apply glue to the base of the back layer of flowers.

4. Slot it into the first slit in the support (that nearer the backing sheet) and fix the tab to the backing sheet.

5. Repeat the previous step for the front layer of flowers.

6. Glue the vase to the front of the support to complete the structure.

THREE-DIMENSIONAL POSY

This elegant card is easy to make with a rubber stamp and some embossing powder. Embossing is a simple technique that gives some really unusual, eye-catching results, but it can be disappointing if it is not done correctly. The embossing powder has to be heated, and the easiest tool to use is a hand-held paint stripper. However, you can achieve the same results with an iron, a hot plate, or even a hot light bulb. The powdered image has to be heated until the powder melts, but it is important that the image is held near to, but does not touch, the heat source. Do not over-heat the image or it will appear flat and waxy.

YOU WILL NEED	
Orange card, 8¼ × 5¾in	Gold embossing powder
Burgundy card, 5½ × 3¾in	Heat source
Clear, all-purpose adhesive	Felt-tipped pens: pink, cranberry, purple, yellow, green
Cream card, 5½ × 3¾in	Craft knife or scalpel
Floral wreath stamp	Self-adhesive pads
Embossing ink pad	

1. Place the burgundy card on the orange card and glue in position.

2. Ink the stamp and print two wreaths on the cream card. While the images are still wet, pour embossing powder over them. Shake to remove the excess powder. Heat the images until the powder melts, which will take 15–20 seconds, depending on the strength of your heat source.

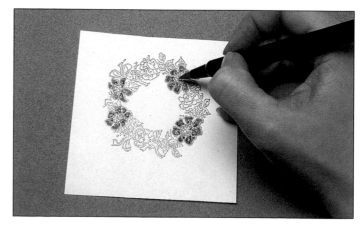

3. Color one wreath completely, using felt-tipped pens. On the second wreath, color in only the purple flowers.

4. Carefully cut out the colored wreath and place it to one side. From the second wreath, cut out the purple flowers.

5. Position the complete wreath on the burgundy card and stick it down.

6. Cut self-adhesive pads in half or even quarters. Use them to position the individual flowers over their counterparts in the full wreath.

PLEASING PASTELS

Lightweight paper can be used to make flowers and leaves. Pierce holes in the center of simple flower shapes and thread them onto 1in of rolled-up paper. Glue them to the gift with some paper leaves. You can make simple tags with coordinating papers, all of a similar weight, cut with pinking shears, glued together, and with holes punched in the corners. Decorate them with small flowers. This simple gift of stationery has been made extra special by wrapping decorative strips of colored paper around the central bands. Add a pencil or ball-point pen, decorated to look like a flower or a leaf, to make a simple gift special.

184

YOU WILL NEED

Lightweight papers in the
   colors of your choice
Pinking shears
Scissors
Pencil or ball-point pen
Double-sided adhesive
   tape
Glue stick

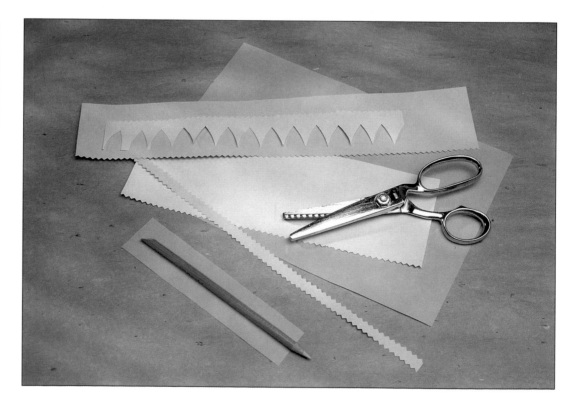

1. Cut several strips of colored paper, cutting patterns along the edge. Use pinking shears to give a zigzag edge to one side of the strips. Wrap these around the gift. Wrap a pencil or pen in green paper.

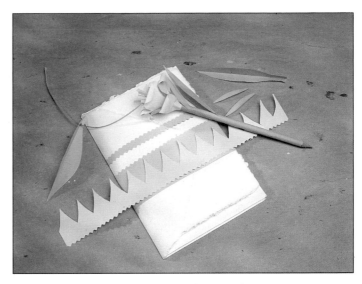

2. Cut out several petal shapes in paper and curl over the edges by pulling them over the blade of your scissors. Cut a rectangle of paper and make a series of cuts into one side. Wrap the paper around the top of the pencil, and curl back the strips slightly to form the center of the flower. Add some larger petals around the edge.

3. Cut some leaf shapes and glue them to the pencil. Cut a leaf shape for the tag and attach it to the gift with a thin strip of paper.

185

PAISLEY PATTERN PAPER

This striking wrapping paper has been very simply made — it is just tissue paper decorated with a simple paisley-type stamp. Instead of the silver pigment ink, you could use white, but the silver gives a pretty, shimmery effect, which is complemented by the metallic ribbon.

YOU WILL NEED	
Sheet of turquoise tissue paper	Silver pigment ink pad
	Floral paisley stamp

186

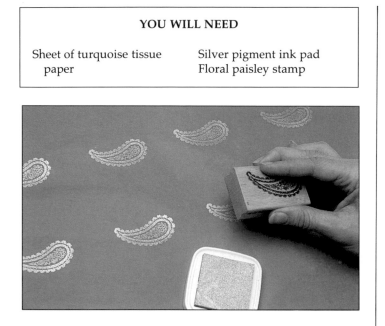

1. Cut the paper to fit the parcel. If you cut it slightly larger than needed, you can hold the paper flat on your work top with small pieces of masking tape in the corners. Ink the stamp and print a row of the motifs, all facing the same way. Re-ink the stamp between each impression. Leave a space of about 1½in and print a second row, with the motif facing the same way. Repeat the process until you have reached the end of the paper.

2. Turn the stamp upside down, and print further rows, positioning the motifs evenly in the spaces between the existing rows.

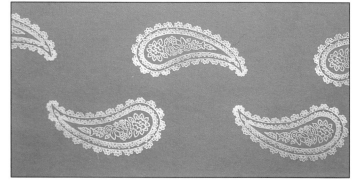

3. Wait until the ink has dried before wrapping the parcel.

PRESSED HERB POSTCARDS

*Greeting cards made from pressed flowers, herbs, and spices are always appreciated,
particularly if the plants that you use have a special meaning.*

YOU WILL NEED

Selection of fresh herbs,
  such as sage, thyme,
  marjoram, parsley,
  tarragon or rosemary
Flower press or telephone
  directory

Paintbrush
PVA glue
Small rectangles of hand-
  made rag paper

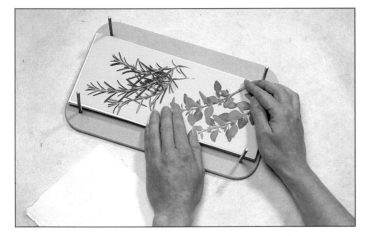

1. Select the best sprigs from each herb and press them in a
flower press or a telephone directory for at least two weeks.
When dry, remove from the press or telephone directory very
carefully otherwise you could damage the delicate leaves.

2. Using a small paintbrush, paste glue onto the herb sprig and
carefully press onto the rag paper backing.

THE LANGUAGE OF HERBS AND SPICES

In days gone by, when messages were often exchanged and thoughts were expressed without a word being written or spoken, the giving and receiving of a small herbal posy could secretly transmit the deepest sentiments. For your card, choose the herb or spice which best expresses your feelings.

188

Allspice	compassion
Angelica	inspiration
Basil, sweet	good wishes
Bay leaf	forever constant
Bay tree	glory
Camomile	energy in adversity
Chervil	sincerity
Cloves	dignity
Cilantro	concealed merit
Fennel	force, strength

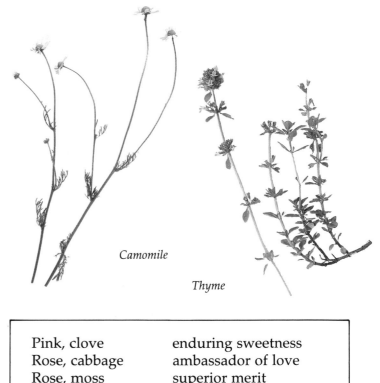

Camomile

Thyme

Pink

Southernwood

Pink, clove	enduring sweetness
Rose, cabbage	ambassador of love
Rose, moss	superior merit
Saffron crocus	mirth
Sage	esteem, domestic virtue
Sorrel	parental affection
Southernwood	jest, bantering
Spearmint	warmth of sentiment
Tarragon	lasting interest
Thyme	activity, courage

Frankincense	a faithful heart
Geranium, nutmeg	unexpected meeting
Juniper	succour, protection
Lady's mantle	fashion
Lavender	industry
Mint	virtue
Myrrh	gladness
Oregano	substance
Parsley	festivity
Peppermint	warmth, cordiality

Oregano

Parsley

SPICE BALLS

These beautiful and fragrant spice balls make a colorful and exotic addition to any gift – not just for Mother's Day, of course, but they would be a lovely adornment on a special gift. Fill a plain brown box with a selection of cooking spices or pot pourri, tie the box with natural colored raffia, and attach a spice ball.

YOU WILL NEED

Florist's stub wires	Sunflower seeds
Polystyrene ball	Dried corn kernels
Snub-nosed pliers	Raffia
Clear, all-purpose adhesive	Dried bay leaves

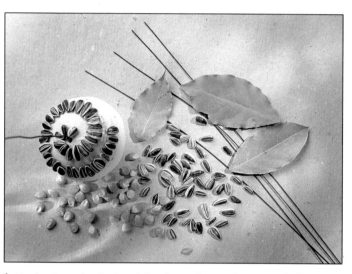

1. Push a length of wire right through a polystyrene ball and use pliers to turn a loop in the end. Draw a spiral of glue around the ball and carefully stick on the sunflower seeds.

2. When the glue has dried, draw a second spiral and stick on the kernels. Leave until the glue is dry.

3. Thread some raffia through the loop on the base of the ball. Trim the wire if necessary at the other end, and turn another loop. Tie on some more raffia and add an extra length for fastening the spice ball to the parcel. Glue on some bay leaves to finish.

INDEX

A
Advent Calendar 102

B
bags 28, 52, 54, 164
Basic Box 45
Blue and Gold 122
Bottle with a Difference 126
boxes 45, 75, 114, 130, 139, 140, 153
Brown Paper Cards 154

C
Canned Christmas Cards 94
cards 19, 21, 23, 25, 32, 34, 36, 38, 50, 62, 66, 68, 78, 82, 83, 86, 88, 90, 94, 106, 108, 110, 112, 132, 137, 144, 146, 148, 150, 154, 156, 158, 166, 169, 170, 172, 180, 182, 187
Cards From Nature 50
Christmas Crackers 118
Christmas Stocking 101
Clashing Colors 40
Collage Star 83
confetti 73
Covered Boxes 130
Cupid's Arrow 170

E
Envelopes 48

F
Fabric Collage 166
Fabric-trimmed Cards 62
Fall Leaves 132
Fancy Dress 124

Festive Fir 110
Flat-gift Holder 139
Flowers and Leaves 169
For the Under-10s 36
Fun Removals 148

G
Gift Bags 54
Gingerbread 165

H
Handmade Paper 46
Heart-shaped Bag 164
Hearts Have It 174
Hexagonal Box 153
Hinged Shell Gift Box 70

I
Indian Ideas 160
invitations 28, 60, 98
Invitations and Take-home Bags 28

L
Language of Herbs and Spices, The 188
Light the Candle 38

M
Message in the Bottle 141
Metal Magic 25

N
Natural Christmas Cards and Gift Tags 106
New Home, Sweet Home 150

O
Oh, Tannenbaum 108

P
Paint Stencils 23
Paisley Pattern Paper 186
paper 76, 79, 116, 131, 134, 136, 174, 176, 177, 186
handmade 46
Pencil Packaging 30
Perfect Paper 76
place cards 98
Pierced Paper 176
Pleasing Pastels 184
Pleated Paper 177
Poinsettia Wreath Card 92
Potato Prints 82
Present Perfect 156
Presentation Envelope 64
Pressed Herb Postcards 187
Pyramid Box 140

Q
Quilled Gift Tags 33

R
Rose Petal Confetti 73

S
Say It with Flowers 180
See-through Solution 141
Simple Bag 52
Simple Gift Wraps 116
Slice of Cake 158
Small Box 75
Spattering 136
Spice Balls 190

Stamped Christmas Tree 90
Stamped Gift Tags 41
Stamped Hearts 66
Start Packing 146
Stencil Gift Tags 43
Stenciled Christmas Tree 86
Stenciled Invitations and Place Cards 98
Stenciled Leaves 134
Stenciled Wreath 88
Strong Paper Bag 52
Sun and Moon Printed Card 21

T
tags 33, 41, 43, 106, 160
Three-dimensional Posy 182
trimmings 122, 126, 161, 165, 184, 190
True Love 172
Turn Turtle 19
Twist-out Cards 32
Two-piece Boxes 114

W
Wax Resist Card 144
Wedding Bells 68
Wedding Gifts 72
Wedding Invitation 60
What a Cracker! 34
Where's Rudolph? 112
Wicked Witch 137
Woven Paper 131
Wrapping a Box 18
wrapping techniques 18, 30, 118, 124, 141